Nelson Literacy

Senior Author
Jennette MacKenzie

Senior Consultant
Miriam P. Trehearne

Senior Consultant
Carmel Crévola

Series Consultants
Ruth McQuirter Scott—*Word Study*
James Coulter—*Assessment*
Neil Andersen—*Media*
Maureen Innes—*ESL/ELL*
Rod Peturson—*Science*
Nancy Christoffer—*Bias and Equity*

Series Writing Team
Paula S. Goepfert, *Senior Writer*
Kathleen Corrigan
James Coulter
Dianne Dillabough
Lalie Harcourt
Jane Hutchison
Christel Kleitsch
Wendy Mathieu
Christine McClymont
Sarah Peterson
Liz Powell
Ricki Wortzman

NELSON EDUCATION

NELSON EDUCATION

Nelson Literacy 5a
Jennette MacKenzie

Associate Vice President, Publishing and Customer Solutions
Beverley Buxton

General Manager, Literacy and Reference
Kevin Martindale

Director of Publishing, Literacy and Reference
Joe Banel

Publisher, Literacy
Rivka Cranley

Executive Managing Editor, Development
Darleen Rotozinski

Senior Product Manager
Mark Cressman

Senior Program Manager
Diane Robitaille

Developmental Editors
Evelyn Maksimovich
Lara Caplan

Researchers
Monika Croydon
Susan Hughes
Monica Kulling
Catherine Rondina

Assistant Editors
Petal Almeida
Corry Codner

Editorial Assistants
Adam Rennie
Kristen Sanchioni

Executive Director, Content and Media Production
Renate McCloy

Director, Content and Media Production
Lisa Dimson

Senior Content Production Manager
Carol Martin

Senior Content Production Editor
Debbie Davies-Wright

Proofreader
Elizabeth D'Anjou

Production Manager
Cathy Deak

Director, Asset Management Services
Vicki Gould

Design Director
Ken Phipps

Managing Designer
Sasha Moroz

Series Design
Sasha Moroz
Steven Savicky

Series Wordmark
Steven Savicky

Cover Design
Sasha Moroz

Interior Design
Brian Cartwright
Claudia Davila
Courtney Hellam
Eugene Lo
Sasha Moroz
Roberto Pagliero
Peggy Rhodes
Jan John Rivera
Studio Montage
Glenn Toddun

Art Buyer
Suzanne Peden

Compositor
Courtney Hellam

Photo Research and Permissions
Kristiina Bowering

Printer
Transcontinental Printing

COPYRIGHT © 2007 by Nelson Education Ltd.

ISBN-13: 978-0-17-629109-9
ISBN-10: 0-17-629109-1

Printed and bound in Canada
3 4 5 6 11 10 09 08

For more information contact Nelson Education Ltd., 1120 Birchmount Road, Toronto, Ontario, M1K 5G4. Or you can visit our Internet site at http://www.nelson.com

ALL RIGHTS RESERVED. No part of this work covered by the copyright herein, except for any reproducible pages included in this work, may be reproduced, transcribed, or used in any form or by any means—graphic, electronic, or mechanical, including photocopying, recording, taping, Web distribution, or information storage and retrieval systems—without the written permission of the publisher.

For permission to use material from this text or product, submit all requests online at www.cengage.com/permissions. Further questions about permissions can be emailed to permissionrequest@cengage.com

Every effort has been made to trace ownership of all copyrighted material and to secure permission from copyright holders. In the event of any question arising as to the use of any material, we will be pleased to make the necessary corrections in future printings.

Advisers and Reviewers: Ontario

Nora Alexander

Stephanie Aubertin, Limestone DSB

Gale Bankowski, Hamilton-Wentworth CDSB

Wendy Bedford, Peterborough Victoria Northumberland and Clarington CDSB

Trudy Bell, Grand Erie DSB

Debra Boddy, Toronto DSB

Maggie Boss, Dufferin-Peel CDSB

Michelle Bryden, Eastern Ontario CDSB

Elizabeth M. Burchat, Renfrew CDSB

Karen Byromshaw, Toronto DSB

Mary Cairo, Toronto CDSB

Cheryl Chapman, Avon Maitland DSB

Cathy Chaput, Wellington CDSB

Tina Clancy

Alison Cooke, Grand Erie DSB

Genevieve Dowson, Hamilton-Wentworth CDSB

Denise Edwards, Toronto DSB

Lorraine Giroux, District School Board of Niagara

Charmaine Graves, Thames Valley DSB

Colleen Hayward, Toronto CDSB

Charmaine Hung, Toronto DSB

Eddie Ing, Toronto DSB

Sue Jackson, Thames Valley DSB

Lee Jones-Imhotep, Toronto DSB

Ray King, Dufferin Peel CDSB

Tanya Korostil, Peel DSB

Helen Lavigne, Waterloo CDSB

Luci Lackey, Upper Grand DSB

Laurie Light, Dufferin-Peel CDSB

Lorrie Lowes, Ottawa-Carleton DSB

Maria Makuch, Ottawa-Carleton DSB

Jennifer Mandarino, Dufferin-Peel CDSB

Carolyn March, Hamilton-Wentworth DSB

Mary Marshall, Halton DSB

Claire McDowell, Lambton Kent DSB

Thérèse McNamara, Simcoe County DSB

Andrew Mildenberger, Toronto DSB

Laura Mossey, Durham DSB

Elisena Mycroft, Hamilton-Wentworth DSB

Mary Anne Olah, Toronto DSB

Judy Onody, Toronto CDSB

Eleanor Pardoe, Grand Erie DSB

Krista Pedersen, Upper Canada DSB

Sarah Peterson, Waterloo DSB

Annemarie Petrasek, Huron Perth CDSB

Catherine Pollock, Toronto DSB

Cheryl Potvin, Ottawa-Carleton DSB

Amarjit Rai, Peel DSB

Tara Rajaram-Donaldson, Toronto DSB

Kelly Rilley, Windsor-Essex CDSB

Joanne Saragosa, Toronto CDSB

Katherine Shaw, Peel DSB

Jackie Stafford, Toronto DSB

Elizabeth Taylor, Peel DSB

Sian Thomas, Renfrew DSB

Elizabeth Thompson, Durham DSB

Bonnie Tkac-Feetham, Niagara CDSB

Sandra VandeCamp, Dufferin-Peel CDSB

Ann Varty, Trillium Lakelands DSB

Contents

16

6 Welcome to *Nelson Literacy*

LITERATURE

7 **Mystery**

8 **Solve the Mystery**
Illustration

10 **The Case of the Sneak Thief's Sneakers**
Mystery Story
by Hy Conrad

12 **The Garage Sale Mystery, Chapter 1: The Theft**
Episodic Text
by Kate Camara

17 **The Dirty Dog**
Mystery Story
by Jackie Vivelo

21 **The Garage Sale Mystery, Chapter 2: The Suspects**
Episodic Text
by Kate Camara

27 **Narrowing Your Focus**
Writing Strategy

28 **The Garage Sale Mystery, Chapter 3: Investigation and Alibis**
Episodic Text
by Kate Camara

34 **The Mystery of Book Covers**
Media Focus

36 **Matching Language to Audience**
Speaking Strategy

37 **The Garage Sale Mystery, Chapter 4: The Solution**
Episodic Text
by Kate Camara

SCIENCE

41 **The Human Body**

42 **Human Body Match Up**
Photo Match Game

44 **Building Blocks**
Informational Explanation
by Melvin Berger and Gilda Berger

48 **Sickening Skin**
Informational Explanation
by Jeff Szpirglas

50 **A Kid's Guide to the Brain**
Informational Report
by Sylvia Funston and Jay Ingram

54 **Bony Framework**
Informational Explanation

56 **Expanding Sketchy Writing**
Writing Strategy

57 **Here's to New Technology**
Short Story
by Susan Hughes

60 **Magazine Messages**
Media Focus

64 **Making Connections While You Listen**
Listening Strategy

65 **Body Works**
Informational Explanation
by Steve Parker

43

SOCIAL STUDIES

69 Early Civilizations

70 Life in Ancient Rome
Illustration

72 Inventions that Reveal Egypt's Past
Informational Report
By Fiona MacDonald

76 Adventures and Inventions in Ancient China
Fantasy Story
by Linda Bailey

80 Museum Visitors Wanted
Media Focus

84 A History of Innovation at the Olympic Games
Informational Explanation
by Nancy Christoffer

88 When We Built the Trojan Horse
Graphic Legend
by Althea Papayanakis

92 Staying on Topic
Writing Strategy

94 Discovering the Truth About Troy
Informational Explanation
by Emily Little

96 How We Lived
Informational Explanation
by Chris Rice and Melanie Rice

HEALTH

101 Making Choices

102 Making Healthy Choices!
Illustration

104 Food Smarts: Myths and Facts
Persuasive Text
from PBS Kids

107 Feed Me
Persuasive Text
from yourSELF *Magazine*

110 Wild About Water
Informational Explanation
by Rohan Siharath

113 Drink Up
Persuasive Text
by Patrick Peters

115 Fun Food Ads
Media Focus

117 Choosing an Organizational Pattern
Writing Strategy

118 Food-Ad Tricks
Procedural Text
from Zillions® *Magazine*

122 Identifying Main Ideas While Listening
Listening Strategy

123 The Right to Resist
Persuasive Text

127 Credits

90

107

Welcome to Nelson Literacy

Your *Nelson Literacy* book is full of fascinating stories and articles. Many of the topics are the same as those you will study in science, social studies, and health.

Here are the different kinds of pages you will see in this book:

Let's Talk
Here's a chance to have some fun and also show what you know.

Understanding Strategies
These pages introduce you to reading, writing, speaking, listening, and media literacy strategies. Some pages have sticky notes with hints about the strategies.

Applying Strategies
These pages give you the chance to try out the strategies you've learned.

Putting It All Together
At the end of each unit, you'll have the chance to use the strategies that you've learned.

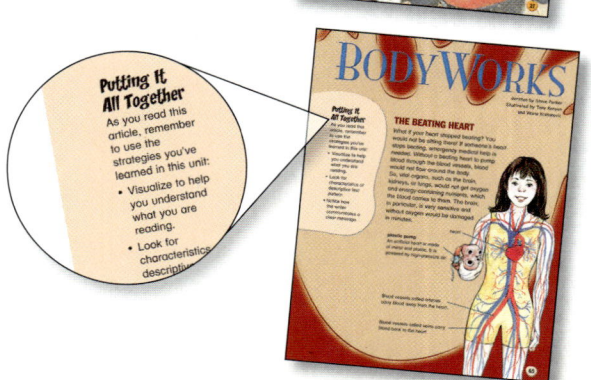

MYSTERY

In this unit, you will
- make connections to self and texts
- identify characteristics of mystery stories
- narrow the focus in writing
- identify purpose and audience in book covers
- match language to suit audience in conversation

LET'S TALK

Solve the Mystery

You're the detective! Use your powers of observation to figure out who the police should suspect.

Understanding reading strategies

Making Connections

Making connections can help you understand what you read. You can make connections by thinking about stories you have read and your personal experiences.

Connect to personal experiences. Think about a time when you've observed something out of the ordinary.

Connect to stories you have read. What stories have you read about characters looking for clues?

The Case of the Sneak Thief's Sneakers

by Hy Conrad

It was Saturday afternoon and Max and Nina were climbing trees in the woods. "Mr. Lee's not practising," Max said as they took a break.

The woods bordered Mr. Lee's property. Every Saturday, Max and Nina heard clarinet music coming from the shack in the field behind Mr. Lee's house.

Suddenly, Max and Nina heard a shout. They ran to the edge of the woods and saw Mr. Lee at the shack's open door. As they approached, Mr. Lee explained.

"Max. Nina. I've been robbed … again! I'd just unlocked the door when I noticed a split reed on my clarinet. I went back to my house to get a new one."

Mr. Lee's music shack had been broken into last year; everything had been stolen. When he brought in new furniture, he bolted it all to the floor—the table in the centre, the chair by the table, even the file cabinets.

At first glance, nothing seemed out of place. But then Nina saw broken pieces of pink pottery on the table. "Someone broke open your piggy bank?"

"It held my coin collection." He stretched his tall frame up to the blank space on his only shelf. "I kept it here."

"Look," Nina interrupted. "Footprints."

Max followed the prints in the dust from the door to the shelf to the table. After that, a jumble of prints led all around the room.

10 Mystery

Nina was on the other side of the shack by a pair of nailed-down file cabinets. "These look like knee-prints," she said, pointing to a pair of round impressions on the floor. "Why would the thief kneel down?" As she knelt down in the prints, a glint of metal caught her eye. Nina reached her arm through the narrow gap between the two cabinets and pulled out a silver dollar. "The thief was trying to reach this," she said proudly and handed the coin to Mr. Lee.

"The thief was wearing SkyMaster sneakers," Max pointed out. "It's printed on the tread. Don't worry, Mr. Lee, we'll find your thief."

Their first stop was Garvey's, the only shoe store in town. Mr. Garvey told them that SkyMaster was a new brand of sneaker. "I've sold three pairs," he said. "The first pair went to Todd Jones."

Todd "Beanpole" Jones resembled a giant skeleton. He played centre on the school's basketball team.

"I sold the second pair to Ollie Infree." Ollie Infree was a known thief whose taste for red suits made him look like a short Santa. He'd been arrested several times but was never convicted.

Mona Everest, as tall as Beanpole but muscular, unlike Ollie, had bought the third pair. Two years ago, Mona had retired from her career as a professional wrestler to breed toy poodles.

"We'll have to spy on them all," Nina said.

"We're not spying on anyone," Max insisted. "I already know who did it."

Whom does Max suspect?

Solution: Mona Everest was the only suspect who was tall enough to reach the shelf AND had arms too large to fit through the narrow gap between the cabinets to reach the last dollar.

← Connect to stories you have read. What stories have you read that asked you to come up with a solution?

The Garage Sale

Written by Kate Camara
Illustrated by Greg Ruhl

Applying Strategies

Making Connections

As you read, remember to make connections to help you understand the story. Think about your own personal experiences and other stories you have read.

Cassie could hear her dad's guitar playing outside the kitchen window as she hastily stuck price tags on cups and saucers. Her twin brother, Connor, burst in.

"Hurry up, Cassie. It's a stampede out there!"

The O'Neills were having their annual garage sale.

"This year it's *your* sale," their mother, Janice, had told them. "You organize and advertise it, and the money is yours."

The twins were turning thirteen in a few days and Cassie had her eye on a new mountain bike. Connor was saving for a wakeboard.

"If this garage sale is a success, we are set," Connor said excitedly. "If not, it's back to babysitting and paper routes."

Mystery

Chapter 1
The Theft

Cassie grabbed the box full of dishes as they rushed outside.

"Mom was right," chuckled Cassie. "Dad's music really does draw a crowd."

Hollis O'Neill, the twins' father, grinned at the customers as his fingers danced over Buddy's strings. Buddy was the nickname he'd given his old guitar.

"Hey, look," Connor nudged his sister. "I wonder who that is."

Cassie turned to see an attractive girl browsing the record table.

"She looks like a movie star or something," Connor whispered.

"Yeah," Cassie whispered back. "She's beautiful!"

Records in hand, the girl drifted closer to the twins and asked, "Who's that playing the guitar?"

"That's our dad." Connor grinned shyly.

"My name's Tori," the girl said. "That's one sweet-sounding guitar. Where did your dad get it?"

"From his father," Cassie answered. "It's been in his family for years."

"Cool."

13

Just then, Cassie looked up to see Mr. Gruffman, their neighbour, coming toward them.

"Don't look now," she muttered to Connor.

"What's all this?" Mr. Gruffman growled. "Once again you have ruined my afternoon with your noise! And why are all these people here?"

"Why does he hate Dad's guitar playing so much?" Cassie murmured to Connor as Mr. Gruffman stomped off to complain to their mother.

"Who knows?" Connor shrugged.

Mr. Gruffman was forgotten when Connor saw the Mackey brothers, Alex and Tyler, blading up the street. The Mackeys lived in a fancy house and had the newest of everything. At school they made a game out of tormenting the O'Neill twins.

"Selling everything we have just to buy a new bike are we?" Tyler sneered at Cassie.

"Get lost," Connor shot back.

"We have as much right as anybody to look at your junk," Alex snorted. "Maybe we'll find a hidden treasure!" The two brothers wheeled away, cackling with laughter as Mr. O'Neill approached.

"We're off to your mom's science seminar at Simon Fraser University. Cass, please put Buddy away for me."

"Sure thing, Dad."

Mr. O'Neill put a business card on the table. "An antique dealer just offered me big bucks for my guitar. As if I'd part with my old Buddy for money!"

As her father walked away, a crowd of customers surrounded Cassie. She put the guitar in its case under the table and moved a box of scarves in front of it. *I'll put this in the house as soon as things die down,* she said to herself.

Ten minutes later, Cassie reached for the guitar case, but Connor ran up. "Cass, Mrs. Filchall just stole some of the jewellery!"

"No way!" Cassie exclaimed, forgetting about the guitar. "Are you sure?"

"Positive. I saw her pick up a pair of earrings and stash them in her purse."

Cassie sighed. "Well, they're not worth much. Maybe we should let her have them."

"I guess," Connor agreed. "Anything's better than confronting HER!"

An hour later, Cassie was helping a little boy try out a wooden rocking horse when she heard loud voices behind her. She turned to see that the Mackey boys had come back. They were wrestling with her old skateboard.

"I saw it first!" Tyler screamed, wrenching hard on the wheels. The boys crashed into one of the tables, sending everything flying.

Cassie scrambled to rescue the fallen goods as the Mackey brothers sped away. The skateboard lay on the ground, forgotten.

"It figures those two would take off without cleaning up the mess they made," Cassie muttered angrily.

She spied her dad's guitar case under the box of scarves. "I've got to get this inside before Dad gets back," she whispered to herself. "He'd freak if anything happened to Buddy."

As she picked up the case Cassie's heart skipped a beat. Something was wrong. It was way too light. Quickly she put the case down and opened it. The case was empty!

Continued on page 21.

Reflect on

Strategies: What connections did you make as you read? How did these connections help you understand this chapter of the mystery?

Critical Literacy: What stereotypes do you see in the characters in this chapter?

Understanding text patterns

Narrative: Identifying Characteristics of a Mystery

Mystery stories have certain characteristics:

- The main character is often a detective who solves a crime or other puzzling event.
- Clues help the detective solve the mystery.
- Mysteries are solved when the clues point to one suspect.

↗

The main character is often a detective who solves a crime or other puzzling event. In this story, two friends start a detective agency.

The Dirty Dog

Written by Jackie Vivelo
Illustrated by Kelly Kennedy

Only one thing could ever have persuaded me to become Charlie Beaghley's partner—boredom. Charlie, also known as Beagle, is the only person my age in the whole neighbourhood, and nothing was happening last March. ==So, when he said he was starting a detective agency and wanted me for a partner, I said I'd think it over.==

When he came back the next day and said he had his first case, I said, "Okay."

So now it's June. School's out, and every day I go and sit in the shed behind Beagle's house. Nothing's happening. I'm bored again. So today I went in to tell Beagle I quit.

"We'll get another job," Charlie said. "Hang around, Ellen. I'll think of something."

> The main character is often a detective who solves a crime or other puzzling event. Read on to discover the problem these detectives need to solve.

> Clues help the detective solve the mystery. Use these clues to help you solve the mystery.

I walked home along the path beside Turtle Creek. At home, I got out my bike and headed for Crooked Hill Road. I was halfway up the hill when I glanced back and saw Beagle, red-faced and puffing, running after me. I thought about pedalling away, but at the last second I stopped and waited for him to catch up.

"**We've got a case!**" he gasped. "Mrs. Thompson came over to see my mother and told her about a dog who has been digging up her garden. She said that if we find the right dog for her, she will pay a reward. Those are her prize lilies he's destroying."

The next day found us combing the neighbourhood for dogs. By afternoon, we had narrowed the list to four possibilities. Only those four ever roamed free in the area. The digger had to be Frisky, Bernard, Brownie, or Fluffy.

By examining the flowerbed and talking to Mrs. Thompson, we came up with three clues:

1. The digger had large paws.
2. The digger was dark-coloured, but Mrs. Thompson had only gotten a glimpse of him and didn't know if he was black or brown, or even how big he was.
3. He had been in the area yesterday, when the last assault on the flowerbed had occurred.

Combining all the information, I made up a chart.

Just one "no" in any of the three columns would be enough to eliminate a dog.

Armed with the chart, we set out to investigate our suspects.

1. Frisky turned out to be a small black-and-tan dog. He had sharp-clawed little paws that would be good at digging. We didn't get a chance to talk to his owner, but we did find someone who had seen him in the area yesterday.
2. Bernard was nowhere to be found, but his owner told us he was a large, brown dog who had been "around here somewhere yesterday."
3. Brownie was, of course, brown. Although she was medium-sized, she had large paws. We were lucky to get to see her since she and her owner had just come home from a three-day fishing trip.
4. Fluffy was a medium-sized ball of fluffy white fur. She had been in the neighbourhood the day before. I didn't get to see her feet. They were hidden under her fur.

← Clues help the detective solve the mystery. Pay close attention to the details, or clues, that the writer gives you.

"Okay, Beagle," I said. "I think we've got enough."

"Which one?" Beagle asked.

"You've seen everything I have. You should know," I told him.

We reported our discovery to Mrs. Thompson, who said she would ask Bernard's owner to keep him at home. Bernard was one dog that wouldn't cause trouble anymore.

→ Mysteries are solved when the clues point to one suspect. Why is Bernard the only suspect left?

Solution
- Frisky can't be the digger because he has small paws.
- Brownie was away on a fishing trip. Since she wasn't here yesterday, she is innocent.
- Fluffy can't be the digger because she is white, and the dog Mrs. Thompson saw was dark.
- That leaves Bernard as the digger.

The Garage Sale Mystery

Chapter 2
The Suspects

Applying Strategies

Narrative: Identifying Characteristics of a Mystery

As you read, look for these characteristics of a mystery:

- The main character is often a detective who solves a crime or other puzzling event.
- Clues help the detective solve the mystery.
- Mysteries are solved when the clues point to one suspect.

The twins stared at the empty guitar case in disbelief.

"Don't panic, Cass." Connor tried to sound convincing. "We'll find Buddy. Just like real detectives!"

"Yeah! Just like on that TV show *Crime Scene Detectives!*" Cassie's face lightened. She took a deep breath and picked up a notebook. "OK, the first thing we need to do is to establish the time of the crime. When did Mom and Dad leave?" Cassie opened her notebook.

"They left around three, and it's now four-thirty. So the guitar must have been taken sometime between three and four-thirty."

Cassie jumped up. "Let's list suspects that were here after Mom and Dad left."

"Gruffman." Cassie wrote down his name. "I think he was still here. He hates Dad's guitar playing so much maybe he stole it."

"Put down Mrs. Filchall next!" Connor shouted. "I bet she did it. She took the earrings and you know what they say … the second crime is easier."

"I know she was here after Dad left. I sold her Mom's old suitcase…." Cassie stopped in mid-sentence.

"The suitcase!" the twins cried out together.

"She could have taken our entire garage sale in that huge thing!" Connor wailed.

"Remember—innocent until proven guilty," Cassie muttered. "OK, we have Gruffman and Filchall. Who else?"

"The Mackeys!" Connor said angrily. "I could see Tyler and Alex stealing Dad's guitar."

"Why would a couple of rich kids steal? They have everything." Cassie shook her head but added the Mackey brothers to the list.

"What about that antique guy?" Cassie asked next. "He came up and offered money for Buddy. Dad left his card on this table. Here it is." She added his name to the list.

Cassie tapped her pencil. "What about that girl, Tori?"

"What about her?" Connor said quickly.

"She really liked Dad's guitar—called it 'sweet,' remember?"

"Now hold on, Cass," Connor protested. "There's no way Tori stole Dad's guitar!"

"You can't ignore a suspect just because you think she's cute," Cassie said firmly.

Connor sighed. "You're right. We have to find Buddy and that means leaving no stone unturned. But I sure hope it wasn't her."

Cassie read aloud the list of suspects. "Gruffman, Filchall, the Mackey brothers, the antique dealer, and Tori. That's it."

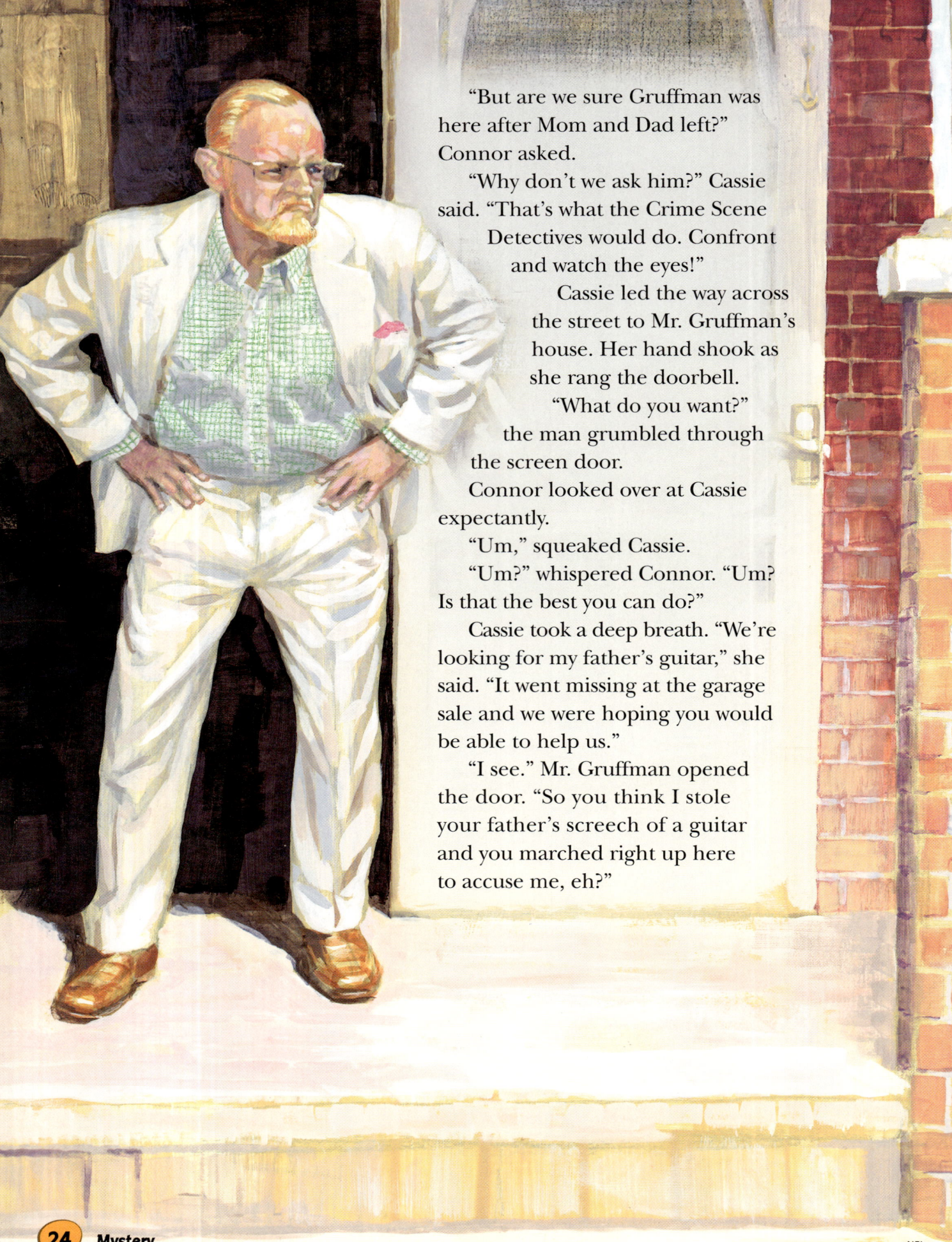

"But are we sure Gruffman was here after Mom and Dad left?" Connor asked.

"Why don't we ask him?" Cassie said. "That's what the Crime Scene Detectives would do. Confront and watch the eyes!"

Cassie led the way across the street to Mr. Gruffman's house. Her hand shook as she rang the doorbell.

"What do you want?" the man grumbled through the screen door.

Connor looked over at Cassie expectantly.

"Um," squeaked Cassie.

"Um?" whispered Connor. "Um? Is that the best you can do?"

Cassie took a deep breath. "We're looking for my father's guitar," she said. "It went missing at the garage sale and we were hoping you would be able to help us."

"I see." Mr. Gruffman opened the door. "So you think I stole your father's screech of a guitar and you marched right up here to accuse me, eh?"

Cassie felt a bead of sweat roll down her forehead. "Not exactly, s-sir," she stammered. "I would never…."

"Stop your snivelling." The man glared at her. "I didn't take your dad's annoying instrument, but I can't say I'm sorry it's missing."

"Can you please tell us," Cassie asked, "what time you left our sale?"

"It's none of your business! I left when I was good and ready. For your information, I took my cat to the vet. Now get lost before I call the police!"

The door slammed in their faces.

"I don't believe a word of it," Connor said as they walked down Gruffman's steps. "We'll ask at the vet's."

"Grab your bike and let's check out Mrs. Filchall first," Cassie said.

As the twins approached Mrs. Filchall's house, Cassie spotted one of the scarves from their sale lying in the driveway. "Connor, look!"

"I knew it had to be Mrs. Filchall!" Connor exclaimed. "There she is."

The twins could see a silhouette moving behind the curtains. They crept up to the window and peered inside. "The suitcase," hissed Connor. "She's just about to open it."

Just then Mrs. Filchall saw the twins. She grabbed the suitcase and scurried out of sight.

"It's her," Connor whispered. "She's got Dad's guitar in that suitcase. Why else would she look so guilty?"

"What should we do?" Cassie asked. "The TV detectives would call the police and get a search warrant. But we have no proof!"

"Why don't we come back with Dad's video camera and see if we can snag a shot of Mrs. Filchall and the guitar?" Connor asked.

"That's a great idea!" Cassie said. "Let's go!"

Continued on page 28.

Reflect on

Strategies: Which characteristics of mysteries helped you read this chapter of the story?

Connections: In this chapter, the characters make a connection to a TV show. As you read this chapter, what connections did *you* make?

Understanding writing strategies

Narrowing Your Focus

Sometimes writers get an exciting idea for a story and then discover they can't think of anything to write. When writers get stuck like this, the problem is often that their ideas are too big or too general. The solution is to narrow the focus, or to make the idea manageable before starting to write.

This writer has an idea, but she needs to narrow her focus.

MY MYSTERY STORY IS ABOUT THE DISAPPEARANCE OF PAM'S PET PARROT, RAINBOW, AFTER MIDNIGHT ON PAM'S BIRTHDAY.

How to narrow your focus:

✓ Begin with an idea that makes you excited to start writing.

✓ Ask questions that begin with words such as "who," "what," "when," "where," "why," and "how."

✓ Write down your idea, showing your new, narrow focus.

The Garage Sale

Applying Strategies

Reading Like a Writer
As you read this chapter, identify the author's focus. Look for ideas and details the author uses to develop her focus.

As they left Mrs. Filchall's, Connor noticed a piece of paper taped to a nearby bus shelter.

"Greater Vancouver Guitar Challenge," Connor said almost to himself.

Cassie's eyes grew big. "Connor, that's it! Tori needed a guitar to enter the contest. She saw the case under the table, grabbed it, and ran!"

"You sound like that ridiculous TV show!" Connor shouted. "What happened to innocent until proven guilty? What happened to Mrs. Filchall having Buddy in the suitcase?"

"Mrs. Filchall could have Buddy—but so could Tori. This says the contest warm-up runs from five-thirty to six at the bandshell in Stanley Park. If we hurry, we can catch Tori there. If she doesn't have Buddy, we can come back and try to film Mrs. Filchall."

"Let's get going, then." Connor jumped on his bike.

Mystery

Chapter 3
Investigation and Alibis

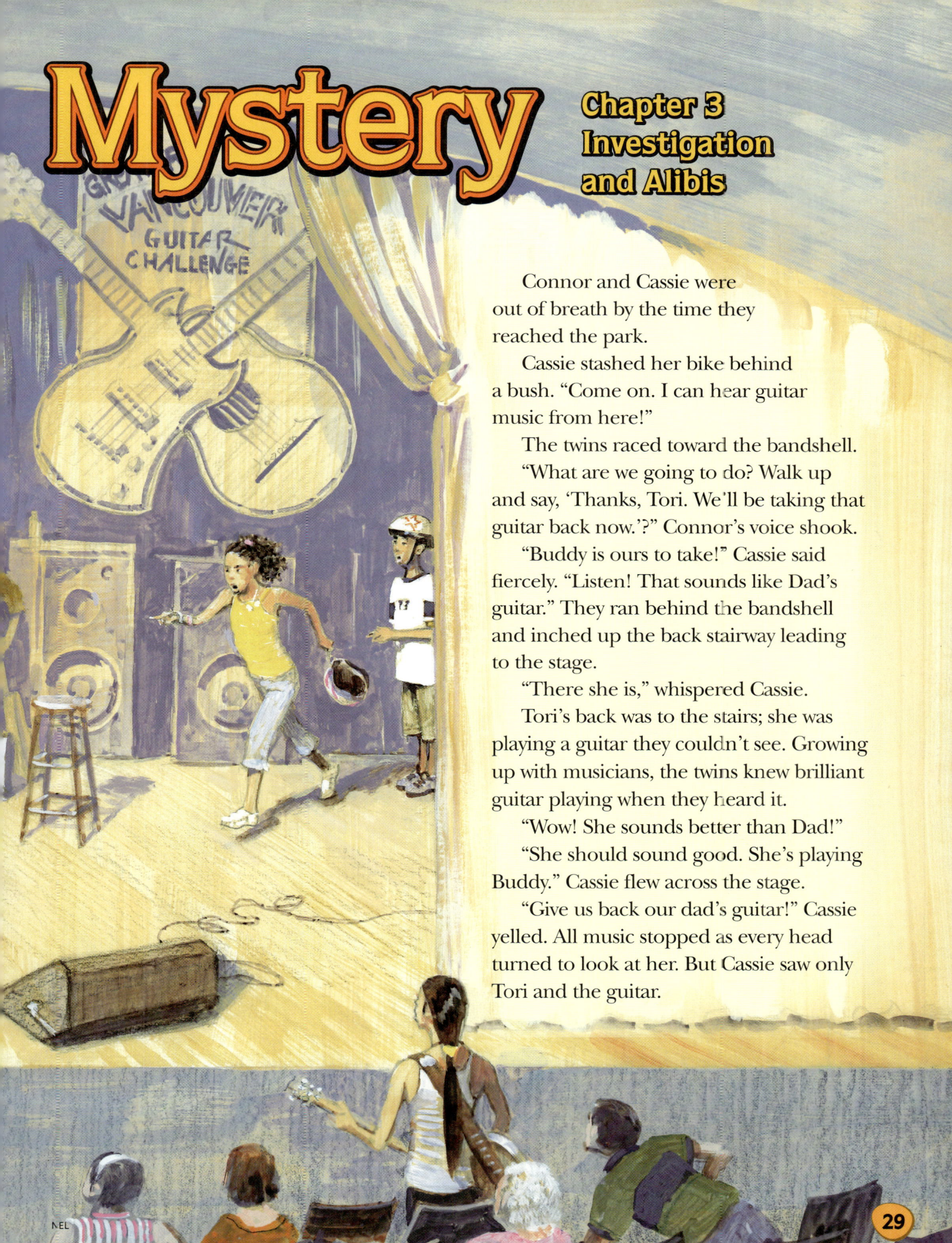

Connor and Cassie were out of breath by the time they reached the park.

Cassie stashed her bike behind a bush. "Come on. I can hear guitar music from here!"

The twins raced toward the bandshell.

"What are we going to do? Walk up and say, 'Thanks, Tori. We'll be taking that guitar back now.'?" Connor's voice shook.

"Buddy is ours to take!" Cassie said fiercely. "Listen! That sounds like Dad's guitar." They ran behind the bandshell and inched up the back stairway leading to the stage.

"There she is," whispered Cassie.

Tori's back was to the stairs; she was playing a guitar they couldn't see. Growing up with musicians, the twins knew brilliant guitar playing when they heard it.

"Wow! She sounds better than Dad!"

"She should sound good. She's playing Buddy." Cassie flew across the stage.

"Give us back our dad's guitar!" Cassie yelled. All music stopped as every head turned to look at her. But Cassie saw only Tori and the guitar.

"What are you talking about?" Tori asked.

Cassie wished the floor would open up and swallow her. The guitar in Tori's lap wasn't Buddy.

"I'm sorry," she managed to stammer. "I thought … you see … someone stole our dad's guitar and we…."

"Come here for a second." Tori led Cassie to the back of the stage, where Connor was standing shaking his head.

"I didn't take your dad's guitar. But, if someone did, that's not cool. Maybe I can help."

"We have to get Buddy back." Cassie was almost in tears. "Dad says that Buddy is the heart and soul of his music."

"We're sorry, Tori," Connor said. "We didn't mean…."

Tori cut in. "If someone stole my guitar, I'd go to the end of the earth to get it back! Tell me what you know."

The twins went over the list of suspects and the time frame. Tori shut her eyes and was silent for a moment.

"I heard the antique dealer," she said, straining to remember. "He told your dad that he would give a thousand dollars for the guitar. It's worth more."

"Did anyone else hear that?" Connor asked.

"Yeah," Tori said. "I remember a woman in a pink shirt looking at scarves beside me and two boys on skates standing close by, looking at baseball cards or something. Oh, and this grouchy guy was sitting in a chair. I guess he could have heard, too."

"Filchall and Gruffman!" the twins shouted. They told Tori about Mrs. Filchall stealing the jewellery and her suspicious behaviour, and about Gruffman's vet excuse.

"I've got to get back," Tori said, looking at her watch. "I hope you find Buddy."

"Thanks. I hope you win the contest," Cassie said.

31

As they rode away Connor grumbled, "I bet Mrs. Filchall overheard how much Buddy was worth, crammed the guitar in her suitcase, and then took it to the antique dealer to sell."

"Or Gruffman," Cassie reminded him. She took the dealer's card out of her pocket and checked the address. "Let's head for the antique store. The North End Animal Clinic is on the way. We can stop and ask if Gruffman came in."

"Crime Scene Detectives on the case!" Connor exclaimed as they pedalled furiously in the direction of the veterinary hospital.

The vet confirmed that Gruffman had brought his cat in that afternoon sometime around four.

"So he was telling the truth about that," Connor said as they got back on their bikes. "But he still had time to steal the guitar. It's a weak alibi, as the Crime Scene Detectives would say!"

A few minutes later, Cassie and Connor burst through the door of the antique shop. Behind the counter was the man who had come to their garage sale.

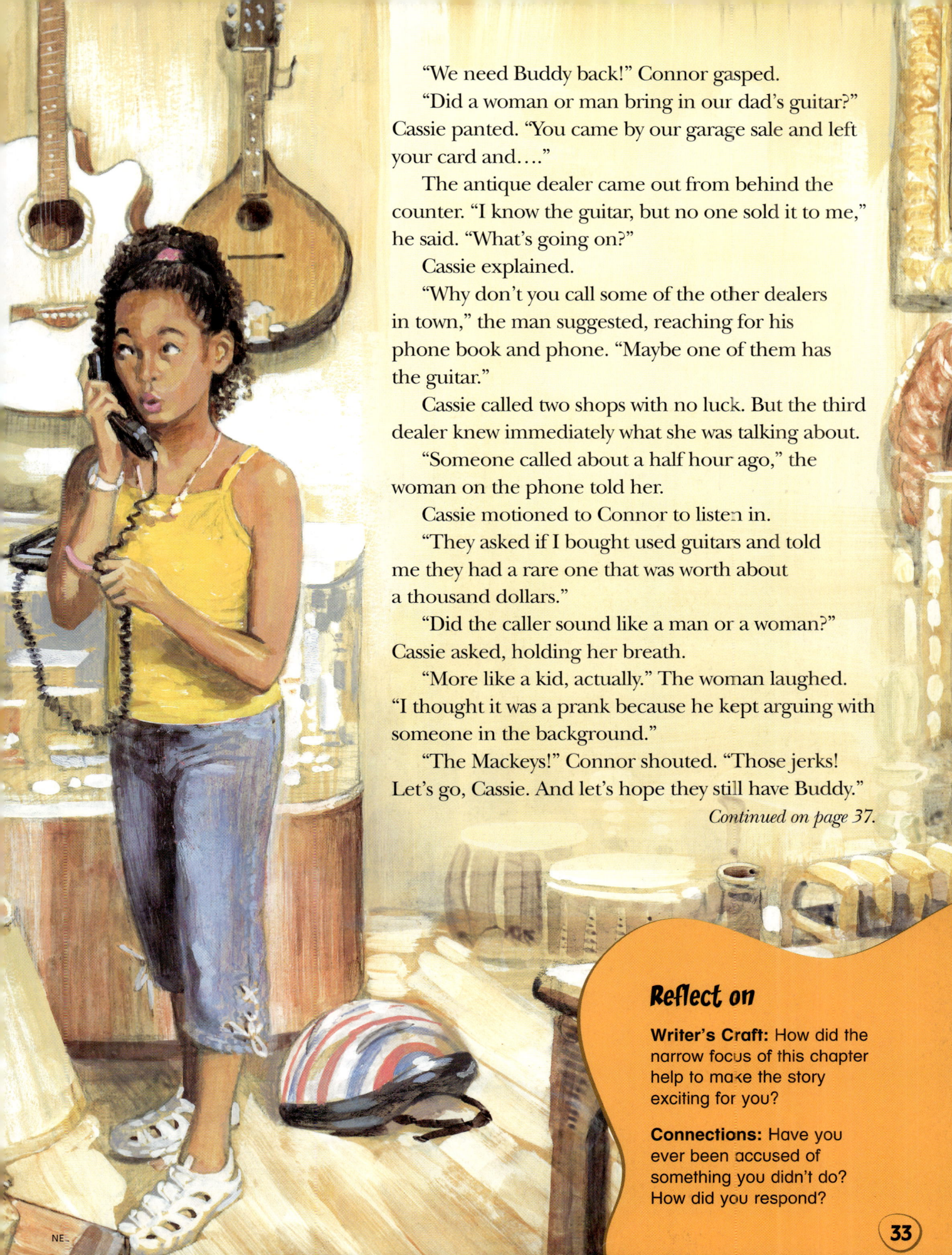

"We need Buddy back!" Connor gasped.

"Did a woman or man bring in our dad's guitar?" Cassie panted. "You came by our garage sale and left your card and…."

The antique dealer came out from behind the counter. "I know the guitar, but no one sold it to me," he said. "What's going on?"

Cassie explained.

"Why don't you call some of the other dealers in town," the man suggested, reaching for his phone book and phone. "Maybe one of them has the guitar."

Cassie called two shops with no luck. But the third dealer knew immediately what she was talking about.

"Someone called about a half hour ago," the woman on the phone told her.

Cassie motioned to Connor to listen in.

"They asked if I bought used guitars and told me they had a rare one that was worth about a thousand dollars."

"Did the caller sound like a man or a woman?" Cassie asked, holding her breath.

"More like a kid, actually." The woman laughed. "I thought it was a prank because he kept arguing with someone in the background."

"The Mackeys!" Connor shouted. "Those jerks! Let's go, Cassie. And let's hope they still have Buddy."

Continued on page 37.

Reflect on

Writer's Craft: How did the narrow focus of this chapter help to make the story exciting for you?

Connections: Have you ever been accused of something you didn't do? How did you respond?

Understanding media

Identifying Purpose and Audience for Book Covers

The Mystery of Book Covers

The dream of every author is to reach readers. They hope readers will pick up their books, open them, and start reading! What makes you pick up a book? For many readers, it's the book cover. The purpose of a book cover is simple—to attract an audience that will enjoy the book.

The purpose of the image is to help readers make connections. Does this image connect to your interests? Who might find this image exciting?

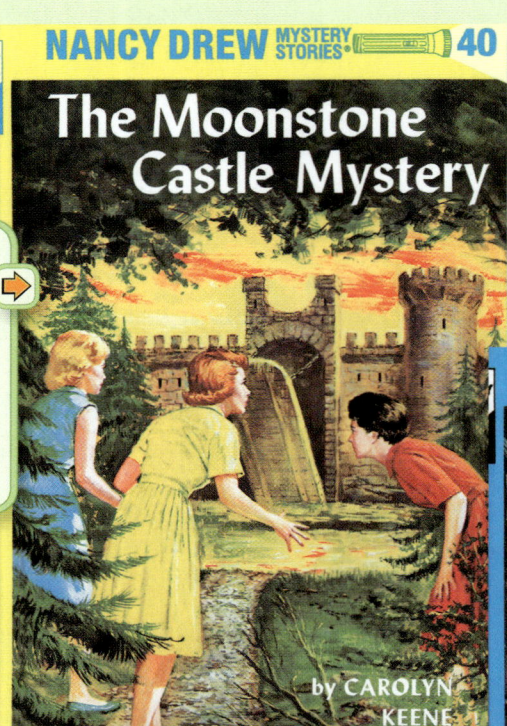

The purpose of the type is to highlight what will be important to readers. Will the audience for this book be most interested in the series title, the book title, or the author's name?

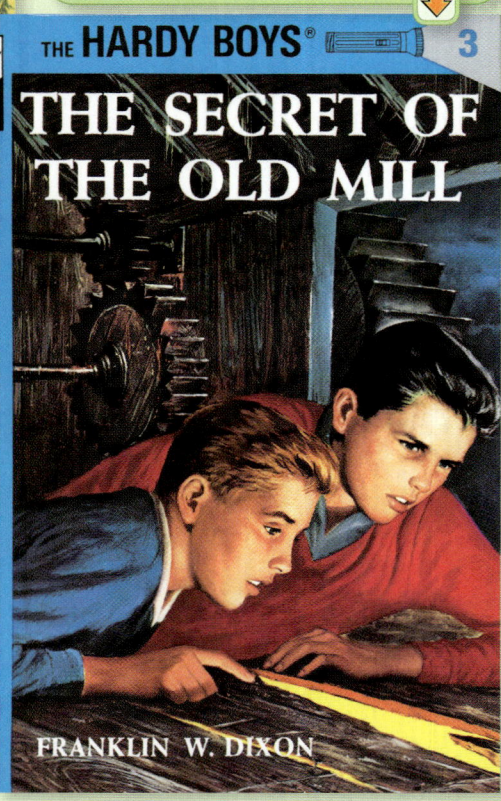

34 Mystery

All book covers are designed to attract readers, but designers use different images and type to attract different audiences.

Take a close look at these two book covers and then look back to the covers on the previous page. What do these books have in common? Why do the covers look so different?

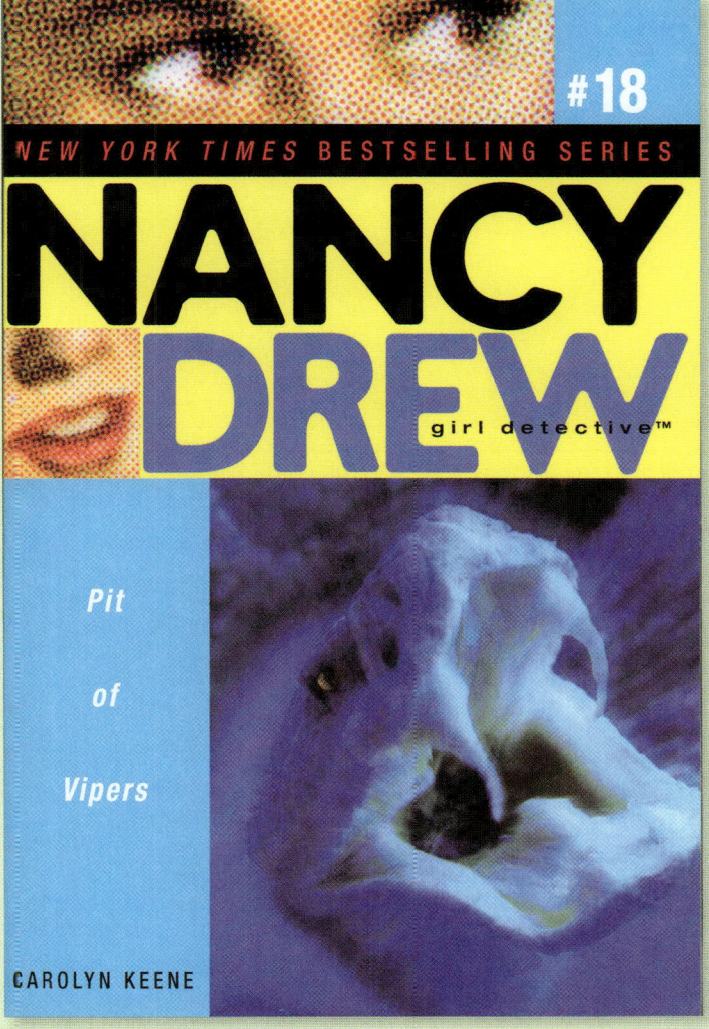

Matching Language to Audience

Good speakers change the language they use and the way they speak to fit the situation. You might use informal language with someone you know well and more formal language with a stranger. Sometimes the reason you are speaking also changes the way that you speak.

How to match language to audience:

- ✓ Think about the person you are speaking to.
- ✓ Think about why you are speaking to that person.
- ✓ Decide whether to use formal or informal language.

The Garage Sale Mystery

Chapter 4
The Solution

Putting It All Together

When you read this final chapter of the story, remember to use the strategies you've learned in this unit:

- Make connections to your own experiences and other texts.
- Look for the characteristics of mystery stories.

The twins snuck along the side of the Mackey house toward the backyard. They could hear Alex and Tyler arguing.

"Let's take it to the dealer!" Tyler shouted at his brother.

"No! A pawn shop!" Alex yelled back.

Connor leapt into the backyard. "Give me the guitar!"

Alex and Tyler stared open-mouthed at Connor. Tyler recovered first. "What guitar?" he sneered.

"Yeah! We don't have your guitar. So beat it!"

Connor clenched his fist and started toward the brothers. Suddenly, he heard Cassie yell from the side of the house.

"Connor! Let's get out of here!"

"You'd better run, Connie," Alex taunted. "Your sister is calling."

Connor scowled, but looked away and saw Cassie pedalling down the driveway with the guitar slung across her back.

He raced for his bike, too.

"I saw Buddy through the window," Cassie huffed as Connor caught up with her.

Connor glanced over his shoulder to see Alex and Tyler blading determinedly after them. "They're gaining on us. Pedal faster, Cass!"

"We're almost home!" Cassie gasped.

Connor could see his parents pulling into the driveway. Alex and Tyler must have seen them, too, because, when Connor looked back, all he saw was the Mackey boys speeding away.

Cassie skidded to a stop, dropped her bike, and collapsed on the lawn, still clutching the guitar. "That was intense!"

"What's going on?" Their father jumped out of the car.

Cassie handed her father his guitar. The twins tumbled over their words as they tried to explain.

"It all started when I discovered Buddy was gone!" Cassie began.

"Yeah, and then we thought we'd be just like those TV detectives and come up with a list of suspects," Connor cut in.

"We thought it was Mrs. Filchall, because she stole the jewellery, and Mr. Gruffman because he hates your playing, Dad," Cassie gushed.

"Mrs. Filchall stole jewellery?" their mom asked, startled.

"Gruffman hates my playing?" Mr. O'Neill ran his fingers over Buddy's strings.

"I guess we'd better slow down," Connor laughed. "We're confusing the civilians." Connor explained how Cassie confronted Mr. Gruffman and about his vet alibi.

"And then we biked to Mrs. Filchall's and she acted all weird and disappeared with the suitcase, so we thought for sure she was the guilty culprit," Cassie explained.

"Until we saw the poster!" the twins shouted in unison.

"Hey, slow down," Mr. O'Neill said. "Who stole my guitar, how did you get it back, and why didn't anyone tell me that Gruffman hates my playing?"

"Forget him, Dad. Your playing is great!" Connor exclaimed. "But you should have heard Tori!"

"We were sure she was the guilty one after seeing the poster," Cassie began.

"What poster! Who's Tori?" their parents cried out together.

"The Greater Vancouver Guitar Challenge!" Cassie shouted. The twins explained how Tori had shown an interest in Buddy and how they thought she might have stolen it to enter the contest.

"Tori gave us the clues. She overheard the antique dealer offering to buy Buddy," Connor explained. "And she remembered who was within earshot. So that helped us narrow down who knew the guitar was worth so much."

Their father looked bewildered. "The antique dealer was involved, too?"

"Well, he was a suspect." Cassie pulled out the dealer's card. "We used this to track him down for questioning."

They explained about phoning the dealers and finding the one the thief had called.

"And then Cassie asked whether the caller was a man or a woman…," Connor began.

"And it wasn't an adult at all!" Cassie exclaimed. "The dealer said it sounded like a kid."

"So we knew it had to be them," Connor smiled.

"Who?!" wailed their parents.

"Alex and Tyler," Connor said. "They stole your guitar, Dad. I guess they heard how much the guitar was worth, took it, and ran!"

"So we biked to their house and Cassie climbed in the window and took Buddy back," Connor said proudly.

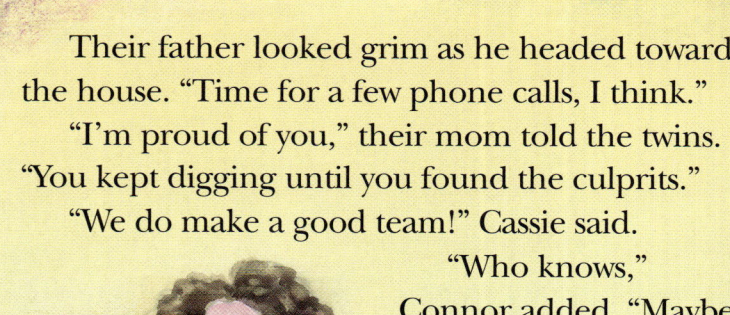

Their father looked grim as he headed toward the house. "Time for a few phone calls, I think."

"I'm proud of you," their mom told the twins. "You kept digging until you found the culprits."

"We do make a good team!" Cassie said.

"Who knows," Connor added. "Maybe we'll start our own investigation business!"

Reflect on

Strategies: How did the strategies you learned in this unit help you to understand this final chapter? What other strategies did you use?

Connections: The twins worked as a team to solve the mystery. What advantages and disadvantages have you experienced when you worked in a team to solve a problem?

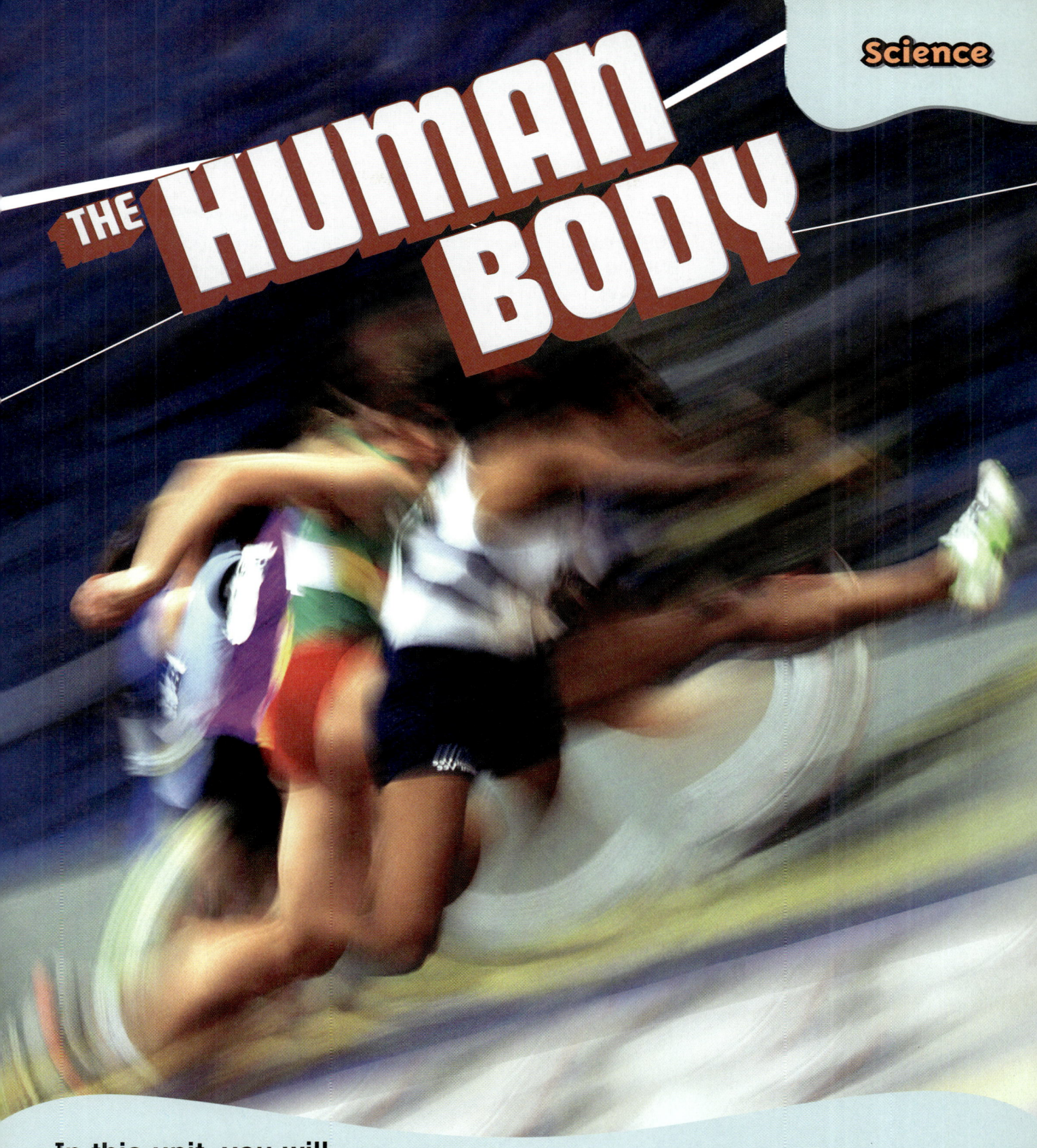

THE HUMAN BODY

Science

In this unit, you will
- visualize while you read
- identify characteristics of descriptive text pattern
- make connections while you listen
- identify characteristics of magazine articles
- expand sketchy writing
- learn about the human body

LET'S TALK

Human Body Match Up

1. stretched elastic band
2. tree bark
3. flowing water
4. bicycle pump
5. computer chip
6. house frame

Match the ordinary objects on the left to the parts of the body on the right.

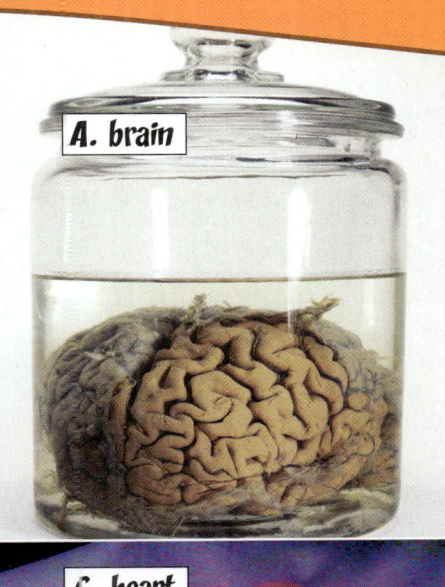
A. brain

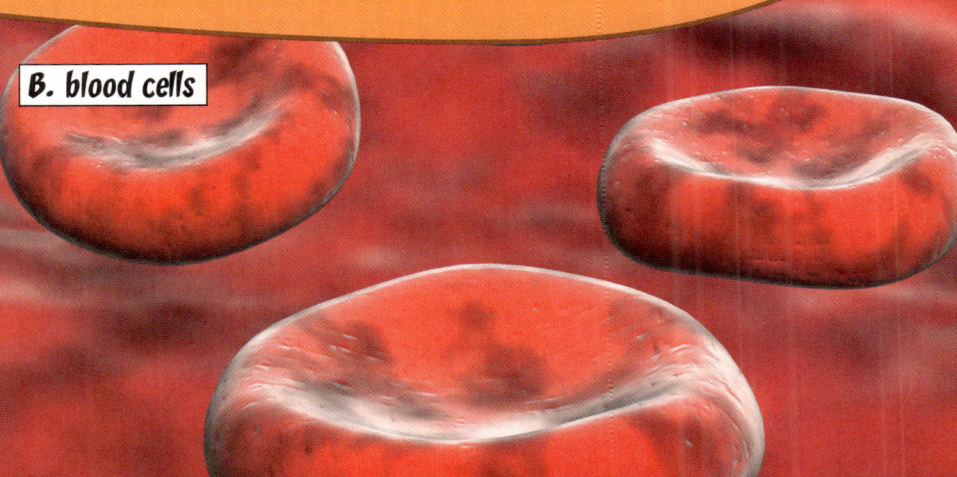
B. blood cells

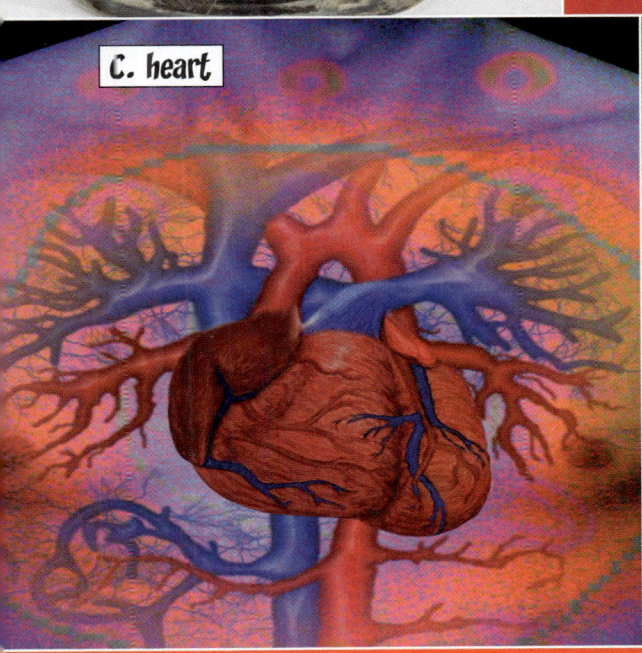
C. heart

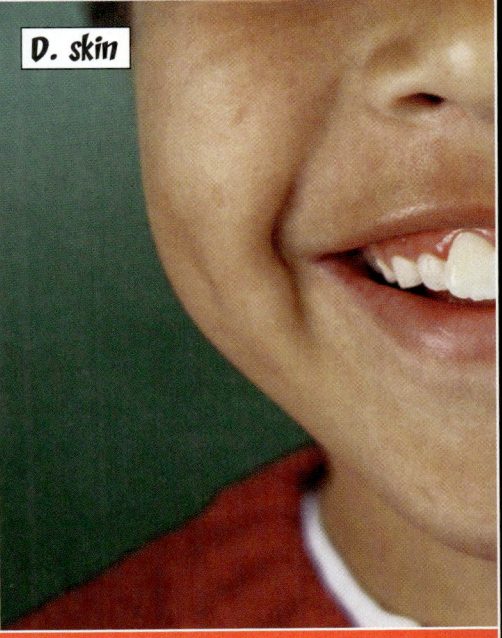
D. skin

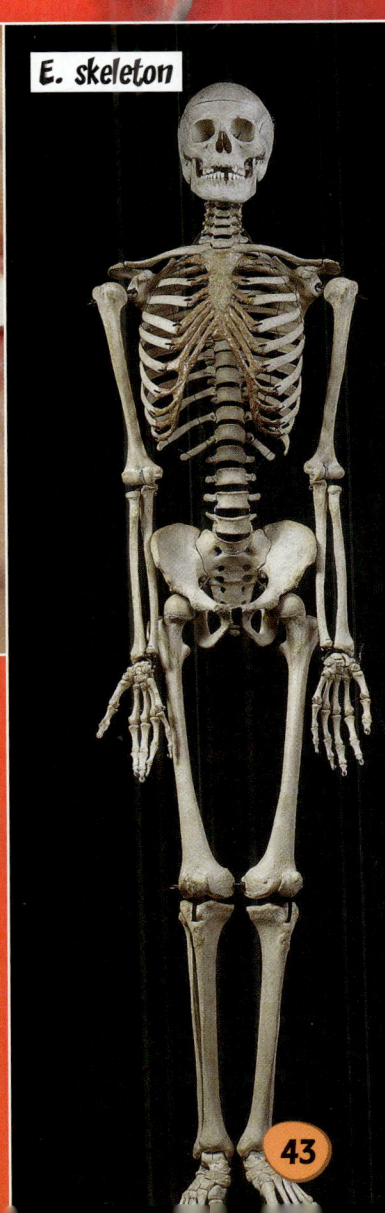
E. skeleton

F. muscles

Understanding reading strategies

Visualizing

Visualizing, or creating pictures in your mind, can help you understand what you read. Good writers give you details to help you create clear pictures in your mind.

Look for details, such as numbers, that help you create a picture in your mind. Thinking about 40 000 cells fitting in a letter **O** can help you understand how tiny cells are.

Make connections to what you already know. Picture an object you know that is about 100 cm long; that's longer than a baseball bat.

BUILDING BLOCKS

by Melvin Berger and Gilda Berger

Cells

Your body is made up of about 100 trillion tiny bits of living material called *cells*. Each cell is a building block of the body. Many millions of cells make up each body part. Most cells are tiny. About 40 000 red blood cells can fit inside this letter *O*.

Not all cells are alike. Cells have many different shapes because they have many different jobs to do. Bone cells support your body. Nerve cells send messages to, from, and inside your brain. Muscle cells tighten and relax so that you can move.

The cells in your body are so small that you cannot see them without a microscope. Each cell is actually alive—taking in food and getting rid of wastes.

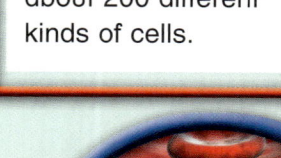
bone cell

Speedy Fact 1
Your body contains about 200 different kinds of cells.

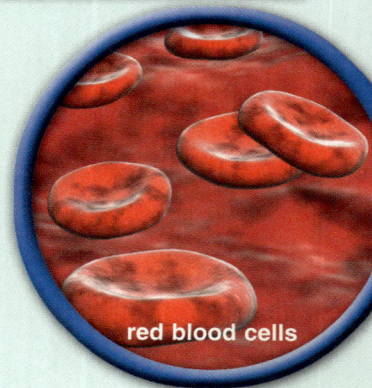
red blood cells

Speedy Fact 2
The longest cells in the body are the nerve cells. They can be 100 cm long.

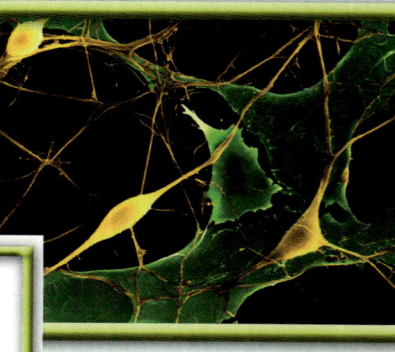

Tissues

Since cells are so tiny, huge numbers of similar cells work together to do one kind of job. Such groupings of cells are called *tissues*.

You have four main kinds of tissues in your body. Muscle tissues tighten and relax to move different body parts. Nerve tissues carry signals from one part of your body to another. Epithelial (ehp-uh-THEE-lee-uhl) tissues form your skin and the linings of your mouth, lungs, stomach, and other body parts. Connective tissues join together and support various parts of your body. Your bones and blood are examples of connective tissue.

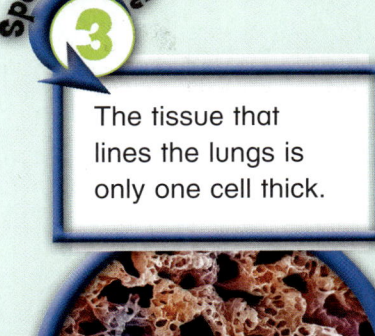

Speedy Fact 3
The tissue that lines the lungs is only one cell thick.

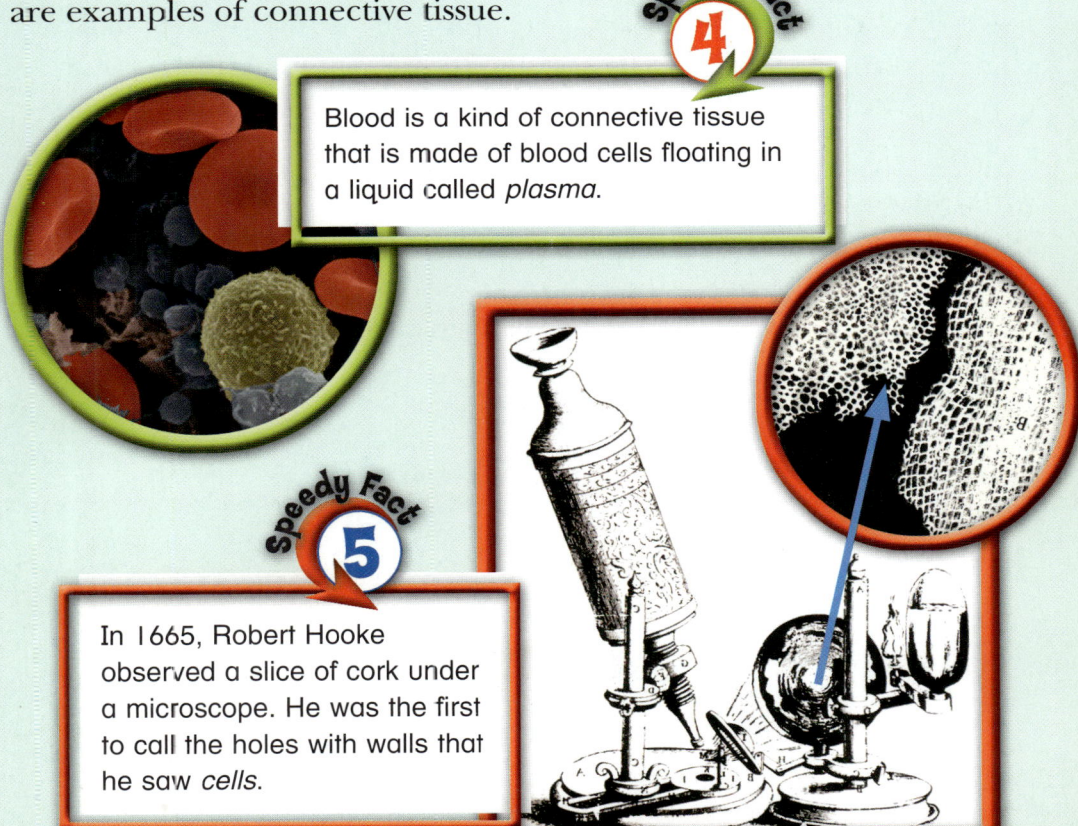

Speedy Fact 4
Blood is a kind of connective tissue that is made of blood cells floating in a liquid called *plasma*.

Speedy Fact 5
In 1665, Robert Hooke observed a slice of cork under a microscope. He was the first to call the holes with walls that he saw *cells*.

Organs

Two or more kinds of tissues that work together to do a certain job form an organ. Your heart, for example, is an organ made up of muscle tissue, nerve tissue, and connective tissue. Its job is to pump blood throughout the body.

The human body has about 50 organs, including the eyes and the skin. Organs inside your body include the heart, brain, stomach, and intestines.

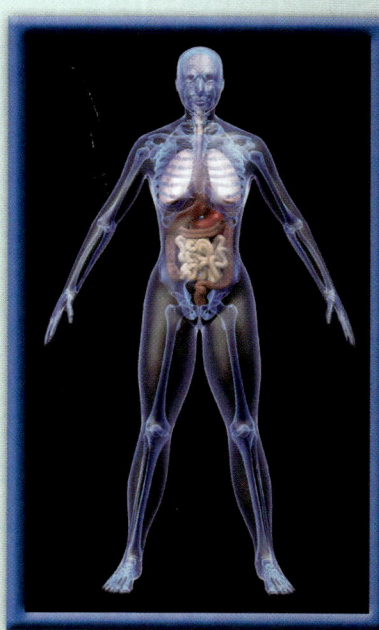

> Use descriptive words to help you create pictures in your mind. How does the word "pump" help you picture how the heart moves blood?

Speedy Fact 6

The largest organ is the skin. You couldn't survive without skin. It protects your organs from the outside world and it also helps control the temperature of your body.

Speedy Fact 7

Some organs, such as the eyes and ears, are on both the left and right sides of the body and look almost exactly alike. When you look at your face in a mirror, can you spot any small differences in how your eyes look? Fold a photo of yourself in half. Hold the half photo up to a mirror so that both sides of your face are exactly the same. Notice how your face suddenly seems different!

Organ Systems

Groups of organs work together to form organ systems. Each system carries out a major function. There are 12 organ systems in the human body. They all work together. Examples include the skeletal, muscular, digestive, circulatory, respiratory, and nervous systems.

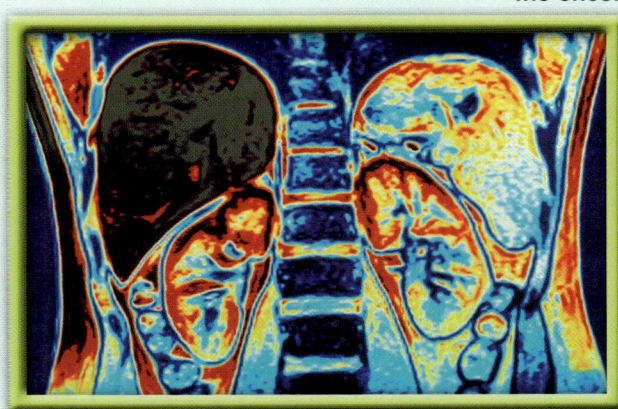
the chest

The digestive system digests the food you eat. Among its organs are the stomach, small intestine, and large intestine. These organs change food into a form that the cells can use for growth, repair, and energy.

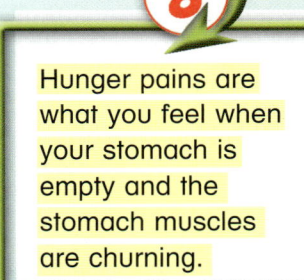

Speedy Fact 8

Hunger pains are what you feel when your stomach is empty and the stomach muscles are churning.

Make connections to personal experiences. Think about how your stomach rumbles when you are hungry. Use that feeling to visualize your stomach muscles churning.

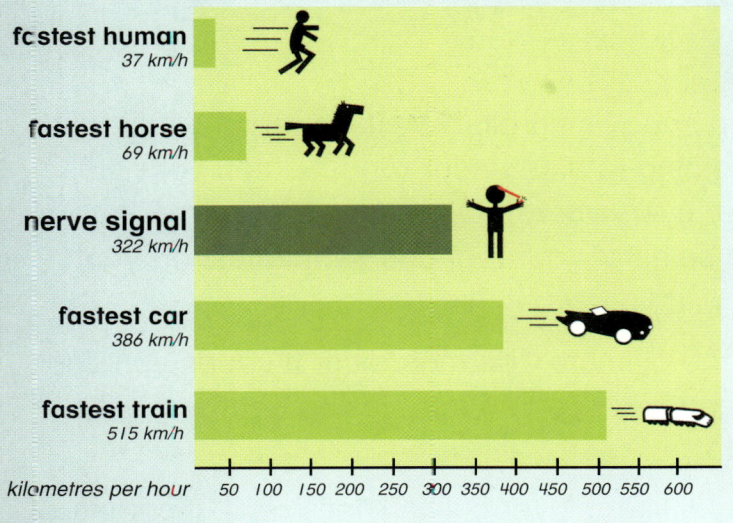

HOW FAST DO NERVE SIGNALS TRAVEL?

- fastest human — 37 km/h
- fastest horse — 69 km/h
- nerve signal — 322 km/h
- fastest car — 386 km/h
- fastest train — 515 km/h

kilometres per hour 50 100 150 200 250 300 350 400 450 500 550 600

Speedy Fact 9

Signals can speed through the nervous system as fast as 322 km/h. That's like travelling in a speeding car.

Use comparisons to help you create a clear picture. The writer compares how fast nerve signals travel to how fast a car can go.

Sickening Skin

Written by Jeff Szpirglas
Illustrated by Michael Cho

Applying Strategies

Visualizing
As you read, remember to use visualizing to increase your understanding.

- Look for details that help you create a picture in your mind.
- Make connections to what you already know.
- Use descriptive words to help you create pictures in your mind.
- Make connections to personal experiences.
- Use comparisons to help you create a clear picture.

If you could shrink down and explore the surface of your skin, you'd find a strange surface like nothing on Earth. Now let's zoom in for a closer look at the two main parts of the skin: the epidermis and the dermis.

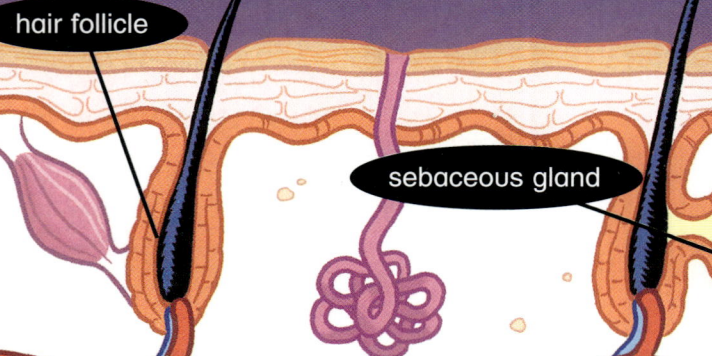

hair follicle

sebaceous gland

Skin is like … a snug-fitting blanket. It's a tough world, and you need something to hide under (and to keep your guts from spilling out everywhere). On humans, skin is at its thickest on the soles of your feet and its thinnest on your eyelids.

Skin is like … the ultimate Thermos mug. It keeps you cool when it's hot, and it keeps you from losing heat when it's freezing outside.

Best of all, skin is like a layer cake! That's right, it comes in layers. The epidermis is the outer layer of your skin. Most of it is made of dead cells that flake off.

Skin Pollution

Here's a little secret: about 90% of dust is made from human skin. Those dusty desktops, the dust bunnies under your bed, even the little cloud that rises as you plop onto the sofa ... they're all there thanks to you!

Dust ...
It's a Gift We Can All Give

- In one hour, humans can shed as many as 1000 skin cells per square centimetre of skin.
- In one year, a six-room house collects about 18 kg of dust.
- In one lifetime, a single person can shed up to 18 kg of skin.

Thank you for your kind donation to the floor.

Dust: The gift that keeps giving.

A message from the International Order of Dust Mites (IODM).

Underneath, an army of new epidermal cells is waiting to take over. Your skin regenerates, or renews, itself from top to bottom in about 28 days.

The second layer is the dermis, which is thicker than the epidermis. The dermis holds sweat and oil glands as well as hair follicles (where hairs sprout from). The sebaceous glands, or oil glands, make sebum. Sebum is a greasy substance that covers your body to keep water out. Yup. You're covered with the stuff. Just try pressing your nose against a window and you'll see for yourself.

Reflect on

Strategies: What comparisons in the article helped you to visualize skin?

Critical Literacy: Think about the title, illustration, and voice in this article. What do you think is the writer's purpose? Who do you think is the writer's audience?

Understanding text patterns

Identifying Characteristics of Descriptive Text Pattern

When writers want to describe a topic, they may use descriptive text pattern to organize the information. Descriptive text pattern has certain characteristics:

- The topic is clearly identified.
- The attributes of the topic are clearly identified and often presented in sections.
- Each section has details that describe something important about an attribute.

A Kid's Guide to the BRAIN

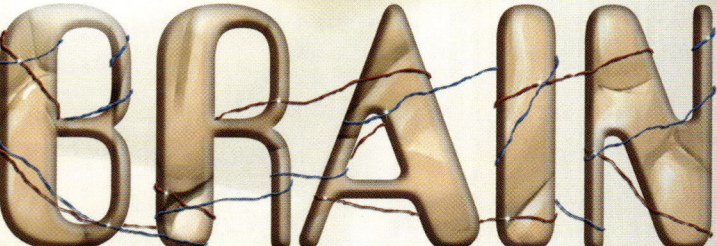

Written by Sylvia Funston and Jay Ingram
Illustrated by Bart Vallecoccia and Jason Bone

An information report is an example of writing that uses descriptive text pattern.

The main topic is clearly identified. What is the topic of this information report?

Brain Facts

The human brain has been called the most complicated object in the entire universe, but you'd never know it to look at it. A full-sized grown-up brain weighs only about 1.5 kg and appears to be made of some sort of pinky-grey jelly.

Just imagine you could shrink so that you were a hundred thousand times smaller and could stand on the surface of the brain. You might notice that the footing is a little soft, but the astounding thing is how weird the surface would look to you.

Brain Structure

You'd be able to see that the brain is made up of billions and billions of brain cells, packed tightly together, stretching away as far as you could see in every direction. If you could shine a light into the upper layers of the brain, you'd see that those brain cells are arranged both in columns that go deep into the brain and in sheets that stack up like the layers of a cake. Every single brain cell branches, like a tree, and every branch is connected to hundreds of other cells and their branches.

As you stood there you would see the arteries and veins that crisscross the surface. They swell and contract as blood surges through them. The entire brain under your feet would be crackling with electricity. There'd be sudden electrical bursts, first here, then there, with each new thought.

The attributes of the topic are clearly identified and often presented in sections. What attributes of the brain do you predict will be presented in this section?

← Each section has details that describe something important about the attribute. What do you learn about the structure of the brain in this section?

The Brain

The front of your brain controls your sense of smell, memory, planning, and some language.

This area controls movement.

This area processes information from your sense of touch.

This area receives information from all the senses.

This area is your vision centre.

This area controls the speech and language centres, some memory, and hearing.

The brain is divided into different areas.

Amazing Facts

- Signals flash between the brain and nerves at speeds greater than 300 km/h.
- One cell in your brain may be connected to as many as 10 000 other brain cells!
- The brain can remember 500 times the number of facts in a set of encyclopedias.

Brain Functions

All that electrical activity zapping around such a complex organization of cells might make you think that the brain works like a computer, but there is no computer that can do what the brain can do. Unlike a computer, the brain can think and imagine itself in space and time. The brain comes already equipped with some of its functions, just like programs "hard-wired" into a computer. A computer doesn't constantly reorganize itself, the way the brain does. The brain creates new information pathways each time it learns something.

Thinking, imagining, learning, and planning all happen in the outermost layers of the brain. The rest of it takes care of many other important jobs, such as keeping your temperature just right or putting you to sleep and waking you up. Different parts of your brain can do these things—and much more—all at the same time without your even being aware of it.

← Each section has details that describe something important about the attribute. This section describes how the brain functions.

BONY FRAMEWORK

Applying Strategies

Identifying Characteristics of Descriptive Text Pattern

As you read, look for these characteristics of descriptive text pattern:

- The topic is clearly identified.
- The attributes of the topic are clearly identified and often presented in sections.
- Each section has details that describe something important about the attribute.

OUR SUPPORTIVE SKELETON

Without bones the body would be as floppy as jelly! Arm bones work like levers, moving our hands out to reach things. Finger bones grasp and grip. Leg bones act as levers when we walk or run. Bones also protect soft and delicate body parts—the skull protects the brain, and the ribs protect the heart and lungs.

GOT A BONE TO PICK?

I THINK WE HAVE TOO MANY RIBS....

ALL THE BONES TOGETHER IN OUR BODIES MAKE UP THE SKELETON. THERE ARE 206 BONES IN TOTAL.

BONY FEATURES

Bone has a hard outside layer, a spongy layer beneath this, and a soft, jelly-like middle section. Some bones, like the backbone, make blood cells in this soft centre. Bone is also very strong and light. In fact, one kilogram of bone is stronger than one kilogram of concrete.

Doctors can also take pictures, called *X-rays*, of our bones. These show if a bone is broken or damaged.

CAN YOU BELIEVE IT?

Babies have 350 bones when they are born. As they grow, the bones fuse (join) together until there are 206 adult bones.

THE SPINE IS A VERY SPECIAL PART OF THE SKELETON. IT IS MADE UP OF 33 BONES IN ALL!

Reflect on

Strategies: What characteristics of descriptive text pattern helped you understand this article?

Your Learning: What did you learn about bones? What questions about bones do you still have?

Understanding Writing Strategies

Expanding Sketchy Writing

Sketchy writing is writing that doesn't include enough detail. When you expand sketchy writing, you give your readers the information they need to understand your message. This writer shared his draft letter to a local newspaper with a friend.

What's the connection between the first and second sentence?

ROUGH DRAFT

Dear Editor,
I like to ride my bike. I wish people would stop idling their cars. Think about the air pollution! It makes me so mad to see them sitting there!
Marcus

Why should people stop idling?

What's your message?

Look at how he revised his letter, based on the notes from his friend.

SECOND DRAFT

Dear Editor,
I like to ride my bike around town. But everywhere I go, I notice parked cars that are still running. I wish people would stop idling their cars. Don't they realize they're creating smog and making it harder for all of us to breathe? Air pollution can have serious harmful effects on people's respiratory systems. It makes me so mad to see idling cars creating pollution for no reason! I want to be able to ride my bike and breathe clean air.
Marcus

How to expand sketchy writing:

- ☑ Make your connections obvious, so your reader doesn't have to guess what the connections are.
- ☑ Explain your ideas clearly.
- ☑ Ask yourself, "Will the reader understand my message?"

Here's to New Technology

Written by Susan Hughes
Illustrated by Greg Ruhl

Applying Strategies

Reading Like a Writer

Expanding sketchy writing helps writers communicate their messages. As you read this story, think about how the writer communicates a clear message.

This summer, just after I turned ten, I broke my wrist playing soccer. I was trying to bend the ball like Beckham when I tripped and fell on my hand. It was a painful break. I was moping in my room when my granddad came to visit. To make me feel better, Granddad told me about when he broke his arm.

"You know, Davi, when I was a teenager, I went to India with my parents to visit relatives. A cousin took me on a five-day hiking trip in the mountains. About two days into the trip I fell and—snap! My cousin and I both heard the break. We were in a remote area, far from any hospital. Luckily my cousin knew there was a doctor in the closest village. It took us half a day to walk to the village. As we trudged through the mountains, I held my arm as still as possible. Every jarring step sent a shooting pain up my arm."

Granddad rubbed his arm as if remembering the pain. He continued his story.

"Finally we arrived in the village. The doctor didn't have an X-ray machine, so he felt my arm, set the bone, and bound it to my chest. Boy, did that hurt! Then we had to go to the hospital. There, the doctor took an X-ray of my arm. He was very impressed. He said the village doctor had done a super job and that I was very lucky. All he did was replace the bandages with a plaster cast. I was lucky, Davi, because I was able to get help, but think about how much luckier you are with all the new technology that doctors use today."

Granddad was right; I was lucky. I guess it runs in the family. When I fell, Mom drove me straight to Dr. Jenkins at the hospital here in town. Dr. Jenkins took an X-ray of my arm, but from the X-ray she couldn't see anything wrong with the bone!

So Dr. Jenkins decided to get some help from a specialist named Dr. Jing at the hospital in Kamloops. Kamloops is about a three-hour drive from where I live. Lucky for me, the hospital had just bought a digital imaging machine. Zap! Dr. Jenkins sent a digital image of the X-ray to Dr. Jing—instantly! The digital imaging machine gave her a better look at the X-ray.

Dr. Jing spotted a very thin break in my bone. She and Dr. Jenkins decided that Mom should take me to Kamloops right away. That same day, Dr. Jing put a plaster cast on my arm. I had to wear it for six weeks before my wrist healed completely. After it came off, Granddad took me every week to the clinic to see the physiotherapist. She gave me exercises to help me get back to how I was before the accident.

Now, I'm playing soccer again and scoring goals. Granddad watches every practice and every game.

Reflect on

Writer's Craft: How did the writer help you understand her message?

Connections: What personal experiences did this story remind you of?

Magazine Messages

Understanding media

Identifying Characteristics of Magazine Articles

Most magazines publish several issues in a year. Readers pick up magazines for interesting articles about what is happening now. The articles in magazines have features, or characteristics, that make the magazines easy and fun to read.

> Visuals reach out to readers. How does the photo on this page grab your attention?

> Different text features give readers different kinds of information. Locate the caption, title, and subtitle on this page.

> The byline and body text are also features in magazine articles. The byline tells you who wrote and photographed or illustrated the article. The body text is the text that makes up the main portion of the article.

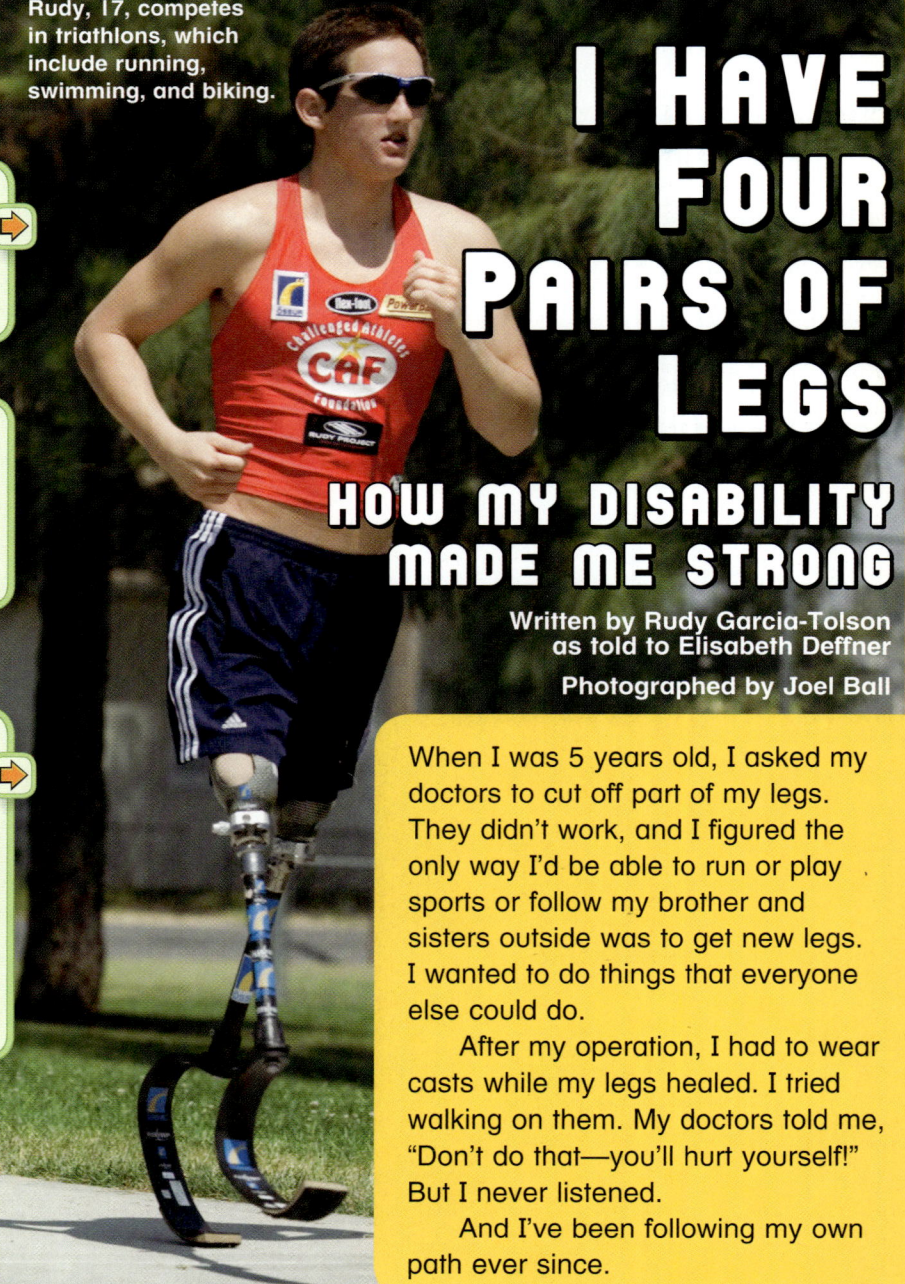

Rudy, 17, competes in triathlons, which include running, swimming, and biking.

I Have Four Pairs of Legs
How My Disability Made Me Strong

Written by Rudy Garcia-Tolson as told to Elisabeth Deffner
Photographed by Joel Ball

When I was 5 years old, I asked my doctors to cut off part of my legs. They didn't work, and I figured the only way I'd be able to run or play sports or follow my brother and sisters outside was to get new legs. I wanted to do things that everyone else could do.

After my operation, I had to wear casts while my legs healed. I tried walking on them. My doctors told me, "Don't do that—you'll hurt yourself!" But I never listened.

And I've been following my own path ever since.

Rudy won a gold medal in swimming at the 2004 Paralympic Games.

New Legs

I was born with pterygium (teh-RI-jee-um) syndrome. All I really know about it is that it's hard to pronounce! Basically it meant that I had too much extra skin on the backs of my legs, and therefore they wouldn't bend. So I couldn't walk.

But I wanted to walk—and more—so I had my legs amputated. Now I wear prosthetics, or artificial legs, to do just about everything. I have four pairs of legs that I use for different activities. I have my walking legs, my running legs, my biking legs, and my "stumps," which are really low to the ground. I use them to walk around the pool or on the beach.

I don't always wear my prosthetics. I don't need them to swim or surf—or sleep, of course! But I wear them the rest of the time. My eight legs are like my best friends. With their help, I can do anything. (Then again, that means I never get out of cleaning my room!)

People ask me how I balance on my prosthetics. I ask them, "How do you balance on your feet?" because I have the same answer as you would: It's just what I do. Sometimes I fall, but I just get up and start walking again.

> Features such as subheads make information stand out in interesting ways. What information do you expect to get by reading this section?

Remember that people read magazines for information—but also for enjoyment! Look over these two pages before you start reading. What feature catches your eye?

Rudy heads out to surf at Newport Beach in California.

A Regular Guy

My family never gave me any special privileges. My brother always let me play football with his friends, and no one ever said, "Rudy can't do that." At school, some of the kids would call me names, but I just pretty much ignored them.

Usually I'm not very shy about my legs. I'll wear shorts, and it seems like I end up talking about my prosthetics a lot. Most people don't see me as The Boy With No Legs. In fact, some kids in my school aren't even aware that I don't have legs!

Sometimes I go to schools to talk to students about living with prosthetics. A lot of the kids have never seen someone like me. Usually I take off my prosthetics so they can feel them. They think that's pretty cool.

I tell these kids, "Don't judge someone by the outside. Judge them by who they really are." I also tell them to never give up. I mean, look at me. I don't have legs, but I'm doing a lot more than many able-bodied kids. For me, there aren't any limits. Why should there be limits for anyone else?

People ask me how I balance on my prosthetics. I ask them, "How do you balance on your feet?"

Rudy enjoys a big wave.

Making Connections While You Listen

When you listen to someone speak, you make connections to your own experiences and knowledge. These connections help you understand what others are saying.

Notice how these students make connections while listening to a commerical.

How to make connections while you listen:

- ✔ Think about what you already know about the speaker's topic.
- ✔ Remember experiences you've had that relate to the topic.
- ✔ Use these connections to increase your understanding of the topic.

BodyWorks

Written by Steve Parker
Illustrated by Tony Kenyon
and Vesna Krstanovic

Putting It All Together

As you read this article, remember to use the strategies you've learned in this unit:

- Visualize to help you understand what you are reading.
- Look for characteristics of descriptive text pattern.
- Notice how the writer communicates a clear message.

THE BEATING HEART

What if your heart stopped beating? You would not be sitting there! If someone's heart stops beating, emergency medical help is needed. Without a beating heart to pump blood through the blood vessels, blood would not flow around the body. So, vital organs, such as the brain, kidneys, or lungs, would not get oxygen and energy-containing nutrients, which the blood carries to them. The brain, in particular, is very sensitive and without oxygen would be damaged in minutes.

plastic pump
An artificial heart is made of metal and plastic. It is powered by high-pressure air.

heart

Blood vessels called arteries carry blood away from the heart.

Blood vessels called veins carry blood back to the heart.

BLOOD RED, BLUE, GREEN, OR YELLOW!

Can blood be green? If it were, you'd probably have two pincers and eyes on stalks, and be a lobster! Not all animals have red blood. In some snails it's blue, and in some worms it's yellow. Your blood's red colour is due to the substance hemoglobin, found in billions of microscopic red blood cells. Oxygen from the lungs sticks to hemoglobin and gets carried around to all body parts.

SMART CLOTS

When a blood vessel breaks, a blood clot forms as a seal. If our blood didn't clot, it would keep flowing from a cut for a long time. With a big cut, a lot of blood might be lost and there would be a risk of bleeding to death! When blood clots to seal a wound, it prevents more blood from leaking out and germs from getting in, so it helps the wound heal. Platelets are another kind of microscopic cell found in your body. When you have a cut, platelets stick to the surface of the torn blood vessel and form a tight seal. They don't do this by themselves. A gluey substance made of fibres sticks platelets together.

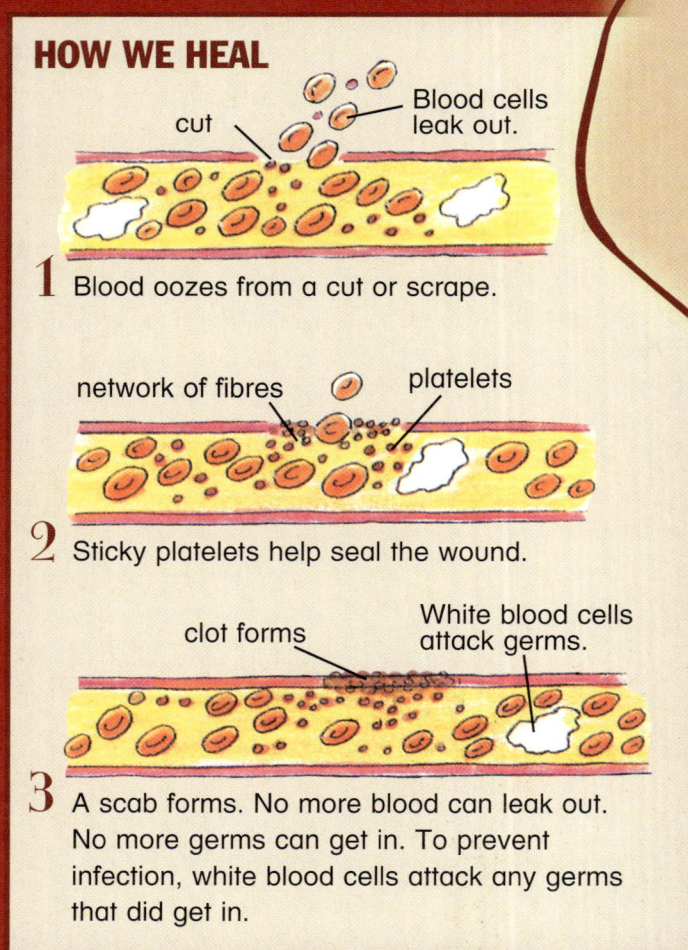

HOW WE HEAL

1. Blood oozes from a cut or scrape.
2. Sticky platelets help seal the wound.
3. A scab forms. No more blood can leak out. No more germs can get in. To prevent infection, white blood cells attack any germs that did get in.

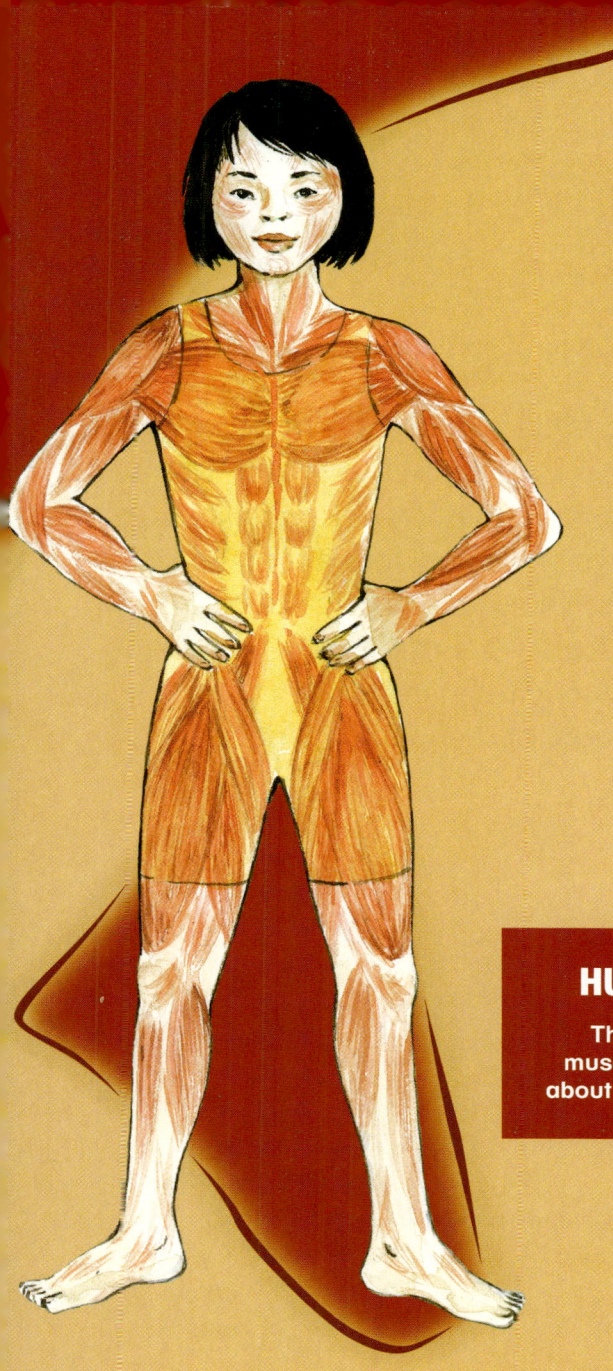

MUSCLES—PULLING IT TOGETHER

What if we had no muscles? You could not tell anyone that you had no muscles, since you would not be able to talk—or move your head, or your arms, or legs. In fact, you could not make any movements at all. Muscles power all body actions and motions, from jumping and lifting heavy weights to smiling and blinking. These movements also include breathing with the chest muscles and the beating of the heart (by the muscles that make up its walls). So, a body without muscles would be quiet and still and, very soon, lifeless.

HUNDREDS OF MUSCLES
There are more than 600 skeletal muscles all over the body, making up about two-fifths of the total body weight.

GORILLA VERSUS HUMAN

Almost anyone can build up muscle strength, by doing plenty of exercises and by eating nourishing foods. But human muscles have a size limit. Our close cousin, the gorilla, has the same number of muscles as we do, but many of them are naturally much larger and stronger. A large male gorilla is stronger than ten 10-year-old children.

Two muscles bend and straighten the elbow. One muscle pulls and shortens, and the other relaxes and stretches.

The tricep muscles pull the back of the forearm bone.

The bicep muscles pull the front of the forearm bone.

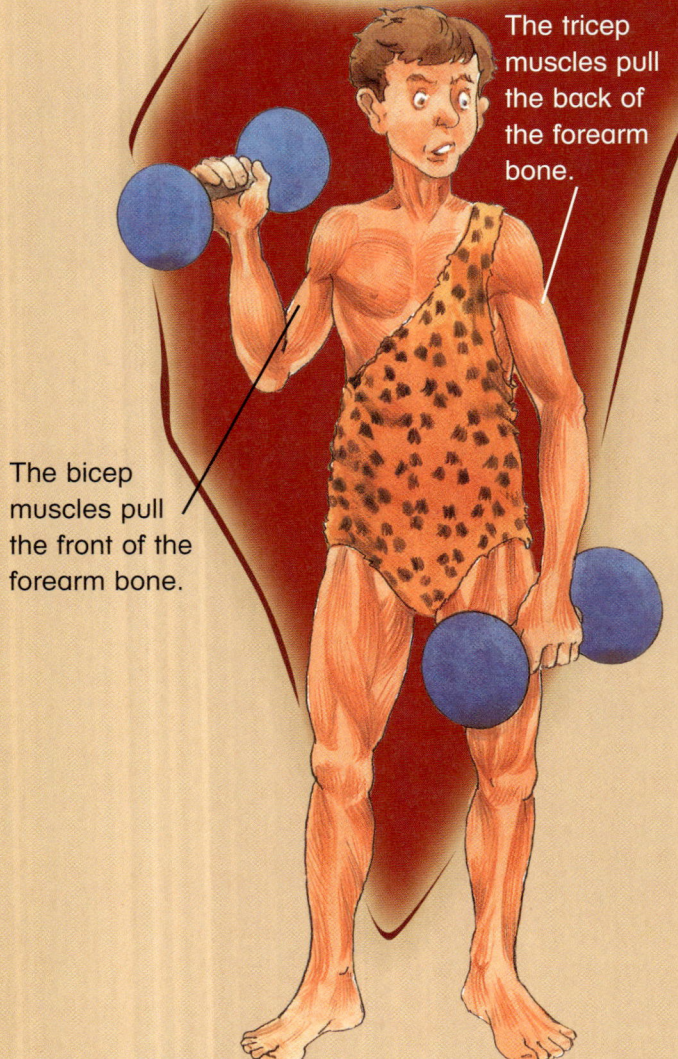

HOW MUSCLES PULL

The brain controls the muscles that move your body. Nerve signals move from the brain to each muscle. The signals flow into the muscles and make them shorten. If these muscles were not under our control, our body movements would be random and uncoordinated.

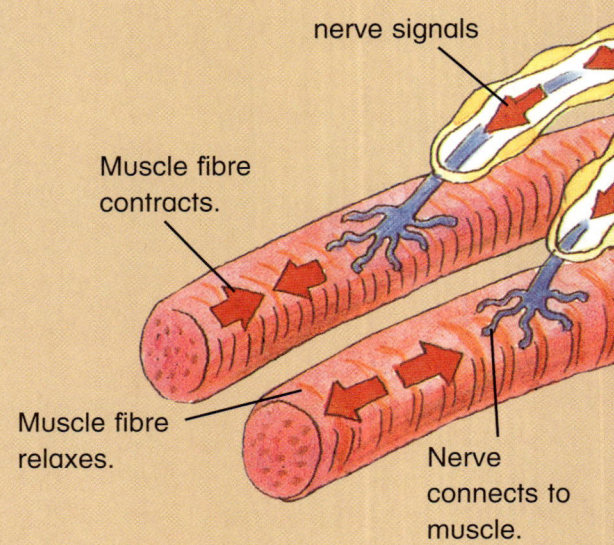

nerve signals

Muscle fibre contracts.

Muscle fibre relaxes.

Nerve connects to muscle.

MUSCLES PULL BUT DON'T PUSH

A single muscle can only get shorter, or contract, and pull the bone it is anchored to. It cannot push. Many body muscles work in pairs. One muscle pulls the body part one way; the other muscle pulls it back again.

Reflect on

Strategies: Find three places in the article where you used visualizing to understand the text.

Your Learning: What did you learn about the human body that you did not know before?

EARLY CIVILIZATIONS

Social Studies

In this unit, you will
- make predictions while you read
- identify characteristics of timelines
- stay on topic while you write
- identify conventions of brochures
- learn about early civilizations

LET'S TALK

Life in Ancient Rome

Early Civilizations

What does this picture tell you about life in an ancient Roman house? How does life in this house compare to life in your own home?

Understanding reading strategies

Predicting
Predictions are good guesses about what will happen next or what you will learn. Making predictions gets you involved in your reading.

Preview the title, headings, and photos. What do you predict you will learn?

Inventions That Reveal Egypt's Past

by Fiona MacDonald

Discovering the Past

Egyptian civilization has fascinated people for thousands of years. The first curious visitors to Egypt came from ancient Greece about 2500 years ago. Today, historians, archaeologists, scientists, and many other scholars use a wide range of techniques to investigate ancient Egypt and bring its amazing past to life.

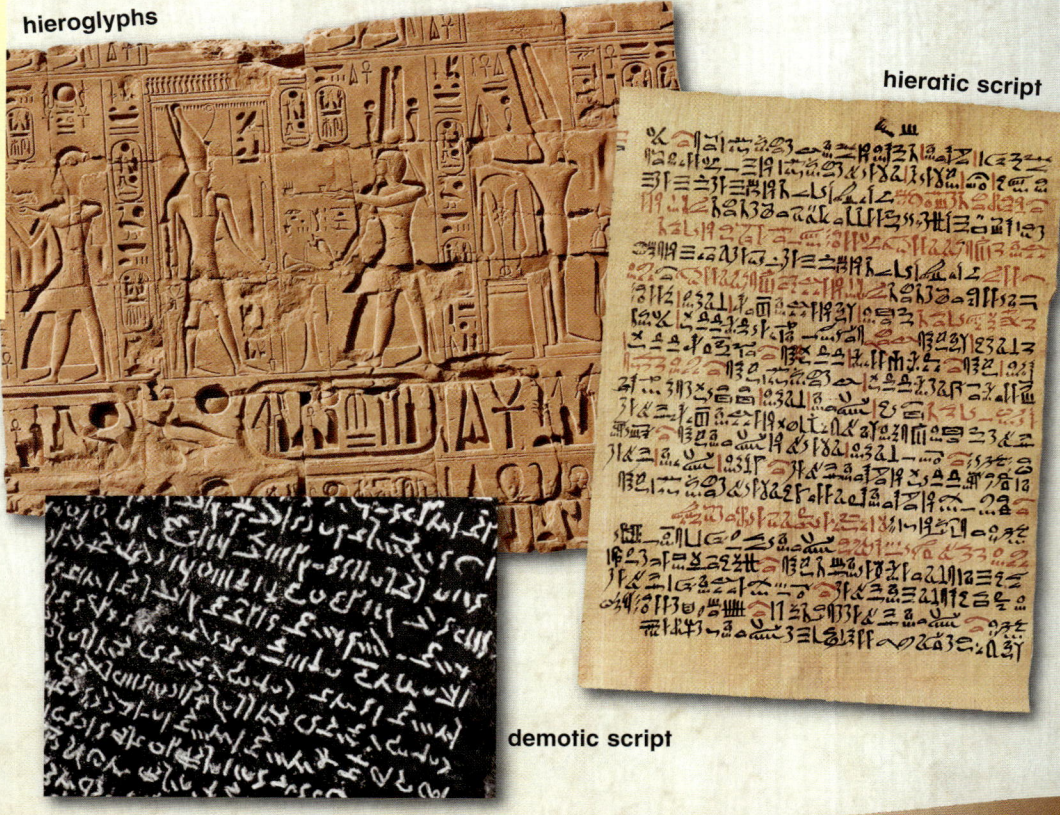

hieroglyphs

hieratic script

demotic script

Early Civilizations

Written Records

One of the main sources of information about the ancient Egyptians is found in their own words. The Egyptians were one of the earliest people to invent a system of writing, and ==many ancient documents and inscriptions (texts carved in stone) have survived until today.==

These documents were created by professional writers, or scribes, using three different scripts: hieroglyphic [hire-uh-GLIFF-ik], hieratic [hire-AT-ik], and demotic [duh-MOT-ik].

- Hieroglyphs (picture symbols), invented around 3100 BCE, are the oldest form of Egyptian writing. Each picture symbol represented an object, an idea, or, later, a sound. Hieroglyphs were used ==mostly for religious texts or to record important information==, such as famous victories in battle.
- After 1790 BCE, scribes began to use hieratic script for government records, scientific and medical works, and books of magic spells. Hieratic was also based on picture symbols, but it combined them with shapes rather like letters. It was written on papyrus (paper made of reeds) with a reed pen and ink mixed from soot and water.
- Demotic script, invented around 500 BCE, used flowing shapes instead of picture symbols. It could be written very quickly, making it easy to use for hasty, scribbled note-taking.

Brief notes and messages were written and scratched on bits of stone or pieces of pottery called ostraca [OST-ruh-kuh].

← Think about what you already know. What do we put in written records today? Predict what the Egyptians wrote about.

← Check your predictions. Which of your predictions were correct so far? What new predictions can you make?

> Stop to think about what you have read, and then make new predictions. Predict what these carvings or paintings might tell you about ancient Egyptian life.

Stories in Pictures

Ancient Egyptians left many clues about themselves in statues, carvings, and wall paintings. These supply details of their clothes, hairstyles, festivals, family life, and religious beliefs.

All kinds of objects, from models of farm animals buried in tombs to cooking pots and children's toys, provide evidence of ancient Egyptians' everyday activities. These clues all need to be interpreted with care, since the ancient Egyptians used a special code in their pictures. For example, green skin was used to indicate life and rebirth. The image of a wife painted on the wall of her husband's tomb might have green skin. The idea was that this painting would help her dead husband be born again in the afterlife.

Archaeologists can find out a great deal about the age, health, wealth, appearance, and even cause of death from the mummified remains of ancient Egyptians.

BURIED TREASURES, NEW TECHNIQUES

For centuries, people interested in the tombs dug in the desert in search of valuable items buried with the dead. Some amazing discoveries were made in this way, including Tutankhamen's tomb with all its treasures, found in 1922. Unfortunately, early investigators often used destructive methods, such as unwrapping mummies, to discover more.

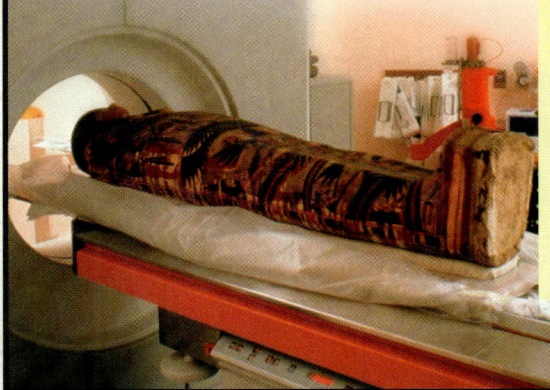

Medical scanners take pictures of cross-sections (like "slices") at 5 mm intervals. A computer then uses this data to create 3-D images, which can be viewed from any angle.

← Think about what you already know. Predict what you will learn from reading about opening up Egyptian tombs.

Today, scientists use less destructive methods. They examine mummies with medical scanners and endoscopes (tiny cameras at the end of flexible tubes). They use microscopes to magnify samples of mummy flesh and computers to recreate skin and bones. They look for buried sites from the air—or even from space. Recently, space photos have revealed the tracks of irrigation ditches (used to bring water to crops) in the desert, forgotten for thousands of years.

RELIVING THE PAST

Stories, plays, movies, and TV programs about the ancient Egyptians have been popular for many years. But more recently, TV companies, aided by teams of experts, have recreated and filmed actual events recorded in Egyptian texts. This has helped us to discover how certain ancient tools and weapons worked, and to get a sense of what it might have been like to live in ancient Egyptian times.

Adventures and Inventions in Ancient China

Written by Linda Bailey
Illustrated by Bill Slavin

Applying Strategies

Predicting

As you read, make predictions to get you involved in your reading.

- Preview the title, headings, and illustrations.
- Think about what you already know.
- Check your predictions.
- Stop to think about what you have read, and then make new predictions.

Josh, Emma, and Libby Binkerton are three modern Canadian kids thrown back in time to ancient China during the Han dynasty (a period from 202 BCE to 220 CE). When they get there, the twins, Josh and Emma, lose track of their little sister, Libby. They travel across China in search of her.

Josh and Emma start out by walking, but they soon grow tired....

When they were offered rides, they couldn't afford to be fussy. Even carts and wheelbarrows would do.

Libby's probably hungry.

I'm missing soccer. I could have been goalie.

She's so little ... and so alone!

Zzzzzzzzz.

My coach is going to be sooooooooo mad.

Travelling by water was faster ... but not much.

Dragons!

Dragons? Wait a minute, there's no such thing. Right, Emma?

Right ...

... I think.

Time-Traveller's Guidebook

Travel in Ancient China

Most roads in ancient China are little more than cart tracks. When it rains, they turn into muddy bogs. Also, there's not much choice in vehicles. You might find a wooden cart and a donkey or ox. Horses are reserved for the wealthy, who ride in fancy carriages. The most luxurious carriages belong to the emperor. He rides on roads reserved for his own personal use.

If you get desperate, try a wheelbarrow. This ancient Chinese invention, sometimes called the wooden ox, isn't exactly speedy, but it can carry passengers in a pinch.

Better still, travel by boat. It's faster, easier, and cheaper than land travel. China has many rivers, and canals have been dug to connect them.

P.S. If you hear the word *dragon*, don't be alarmed. Dragons are not scary here. The Chinese think of dragons as wise, good, and strong. They believe that dragons are rain spirits who live in lakes, rivers, seas, and rain clouds.

Josh and Emma were desperate to find Libby. But it had been a long time since lunch. Stopping at the next farm, the twins offered to work the water wheel in return for food.

"I feel like a hamster."

"I'm hungry enough to *eat* a hamster. Pedal!"

Chinese Inventions

The ancient Chinese are great inventors. You've already discovered one of their inventions—the wheelbarrow. It may not look like much, but it makes moving loads a lot easier. And if you want to move water, why not try the dragon's backbone? You just pedal an endless chain of wooden planks to lift the water uphill. Excellent for watering the crops!

Not impressed yet? The Chinese also discovered that if you attach a lodestone (magnetic rock) to a wooden fish and float it in water, the fish will point north–south. Presto—the first compass!

Or how about a seismograph? China is a land of earthquakes, and a brilliant Han scientist (Zhang Heng) invented a seismograph, a device to record earthquake activity.

Still not impressed? Well, what are you holding in your hands? Paper! Chinese invention. Printing! Another Chinese invention. How about umbrellas, kites, fishing reels, mechanical clocks, and water wheels? All Chinese inventions! You may have to hang around a few years (say, 800) to see the Chinese invent gunpowder and fireworks....

But hey! What's your hurry?

78 Early Civilizations

Day after day, Josh and Emma trudged north in their sister's tracks. One day, they stumbled across some people making paper.

Writing and Paper

The Chinese began writing around 1300 BCE. They began by drawing pictograms (small pictures). Over time, there were more and more pictograms, which got more and more complicated. Thousands of different characters make up the Chinese written language.

At first, the Chinese wrote on turtle shells, bones, and bronze vessels. Later, they wrote on strips of bamboo. These strips were read up and down and tied together with string to make a book. Important messages would be written on silk instead. (Very expensive! Not for first drafts.)

Paper was invented in the Han dynasty. Credit is given to an official named Cai Lun in 105 CE, but he probably just improved the process. The first papermakers used old rags to make their paper. Later, they experimented with mulberry bark, rattan, bamboo, and even fish nets.

Take a good look at the paper they're making in this scene. It's one of the most important inventions ever. It will be hundreds of years before the rest of the world catches on!

Will Josh and Emma ever find Libby? To read their entire adventure, look for Linda Bailey's book *Adventures in Ancient China*.

Reflect on

Strategies: What predictions did you make while you were reading? How did these predictions help you get involved in your reading?

Your Learning: Which inventions of the ancient Chinese would you like to tell someone about? Look back to remind yourself of the facts.

Understanding media

Museum Visitors Wanted

Identifying Conventions of Brochures

Many different organizations want you to know about them. They want to tell you who they are, what they do, what they sell, where they are, and why you should spend money on them.

One of the most common ways of getting the message out to you is to design and produce a brochure. A brochure is usually a single sheet of paper, printed on both sides, and folded into thirds. Each "third" is called a panel. A brochure folded in thirds has six panels, and each panel is like a new page.

> The first panel of a brochure tells who produced it and grabs the reader's attention, like a book cover does. What makes you want to look inside this brochure?

Worlds to Explore

Explore the world at the Royal Ontario Museum in Toronto. Numbering six million objects, the ROM's renowned collections reflect both world cultures and natural history. From Egyptian mummies and medieval armour, to the biodiversity of the natural world, there's something new to discover around every corner.

Great Expectations

In 2007, the Michael Lee-Chin Crystal was unveiled, completing the spectacular transformation of the ROM. Designed by Daniel Libeskind, this unique building will include galleries of dinosaurs; fossils, minerals, and gems; costumes and textiles; 20th-century design; world cultures from around the globe; a new Institute for Contemporary Culture; and more. Enjoy exciting international exhibitions, three new restaurants, and world-class shopping.

> A brochure has clear organization and tightly packed information. The middle panel tells you what the ROM is. What do you learn in the third panel?

> Photos and illustrations create excitement and provide information. How are photos used on the first three panels?

> Brochures are usually written for adults. Who do you think this brochure is for? How can you tell?

When you pick up a brochure, you get a strong first impression of the organization that created it. This brochure from the Royal Ontario Museum is printed in colour on thick, glossy paper. What impression do you think the museum wants to make on you?

As you read these panels of the ROM brochure, identify the conventions of brochures:

- A brochure has clear organization and tightly packed information.
- Photos and illustrations create excitement and provide information.

If a brochure has done its job, readers want to tuck it in their pocket so they can refer to it later. What parts of this brochure would make you want to save it?

Old Favourites

- **Galleries of Africa: Egypt**, filled with mummy cases, scar seals and more
- **Gallery of Greece**, including pottery and portraits, fresco and figurines from this fascinating ancient culture
- **Evolution of Style**, a gallery tracing trends in art from the Renaissance to Art Deco
- **Arms and Armour**, the largest collection of its kind in Can
- **Hands-on Biodiversity**, a favourite with young nature love
- **Gallery of Mammals**, with lions, tigers and rainforest chi
- **Gallery of Birds**, featuring hundreds of different species birds, shown together in one flock
- **Bat Cave**, a dark grotto of bats, snakes and creepy craw
- **ROM Reproductions**, the Museum's shop, selling exquisite replicas inspired by the ROM's collections
- Plus much more!

Early Civilizations

10 New Galleries

Now Open

...ey and Toby Tanenbaum Gallery of China, one of the ...ost important collections of Chinese art outside of China

...OM Gallery of Chinese Architecture, North America's first, ...aturing a brilliantly painted Imperial Palace reconstruction

...shop White Gallery of Chinese Temple Art, the world's ...est-preserved 14th-century temple wall paintings

...atthews Family Court of Chinese Sculpture, 2000 years ... Chinese religious art

...ince Takamado Gallery of Japan, the largest collection ... Japanese art in Canada

...allery of Korea, Canada's only permanent gallery ...edicated to Korean art and culture

...erman Herzog Levy Gallery, a showcase for temporary ...r Eastern exhibitions

...allery of Canada: First Peoples, aboriginal cultures ...xplored through both living artists and historical works

...allery of the Bronze Age Aegean, ancient pre-classical ...t and culture

...G. Leventis Foundation Gallery of Ancient Cyprus, artifacts ...om the Bronze Age through to the Hellenistic period

Visitor Information

Contact Us
Switchboard: 416.586.5549
24-Hour Recorded Information: 416.586.8000
Group Bookings (10 or more people): 416.586.5859
School Bookings: 416.586.5801
Become a Member and visit for free!: 416.586.5700
Book a Special Event: 416.586.5572
ROMLife and ROMkids programs: 416.586.5797
Bell Relay Service for People who are Deaf (TTY/TDY): 711

Hours
Open Daily 10 am to 6 pm
Fridays until 9:30 pm
Closed Dec. 25 and Jan. 1

Admission Prices
Admission prices change with exhibition schedules.
Please call the switchboard or visit our website for current rates.

Tickets
Available on our website or in person at the ROM. For a great deal, purchase a CityPass for admission to six Toronto attractions including the Royal Ontario Museum, for one low price! Available at the ROM or on our website.

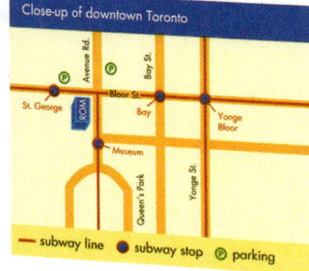
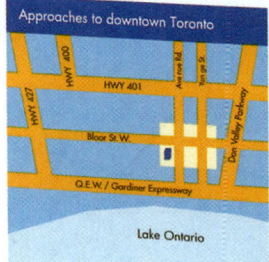

 **Royal Ontario Museum**
World Cultures | Natural History

Bloor St. W. at Avenue Rd.
Museum subway stop
Toronto, Ontario

Royal Ontario Museum, 100 Queen's Park, Toronto, Ontario, Canada, M5S 2C6. Architectural rendering by Miller Hare.
All images © Royal Ontario Museum, 2005. All rights reserved. The ROM is an agency of the Government of Ontario.
Pour des renseignements en français, composez le 416.586.8000. Printed in Canada, 12/05.

Understanding reading strategies

Text Features: Timelines

A timeline shows key events in the order they happened. A timeline
- gives a date for each event
- shows key events in order
- shows the earliest event at the beginning and the most recent event at the end

A HISTORY OF INNOVATION AT THE OLYMPIC GAMES

by Nancy Christoffer

A timeline gives a date for each event. What are the dates of the three events shown on this page? →

Ancient Greece
The Olympic Games begin as a religious festival. They are held every four years. The Games bring together people from many places. It is a time to worship, compete, and trade in peace.

before 776 BCE

Olympia, Greece
The Olympics is noted for the first time in written records. Women are not allowed to compete in the Olympics. Instead, they compete in their own Hera Games.

776 BCE

Olympia, Greece
Roman Emperor Nero competes. Contestants are afraid to challenge this powerful leader. Thus, Nero wins all events he enters. Poetry is introduced as an event.

67 CE

84 Early Civilizations

Olympic Facts

- The Olympic motto is a Latin phrase that means "swifter, higher, stronger."
- The five rings of the Olympic flag symbolize unity. Each coloured ring represents at least one colour in the flag of most nations.
- The torch relay, Olympic flame, and Olympic oath have been part of the Games since ancient times.

Olympia, Greece
Roman Emperor Theodosius bans certain festivals, including the Olympic Games.

Athens, Greece
Baron Pierre de Coubertin revives the Olympics to increase international understanding and goodwill. Fourteen countries are represented. About 245 men compete in 43 events.

Paris, France
Women are allowed to compete in golf, tennis, and croquet. Men compete in 75 events.

394   1896   1900

A timeline shows key events in order. What key event in 1900 do you find out about?

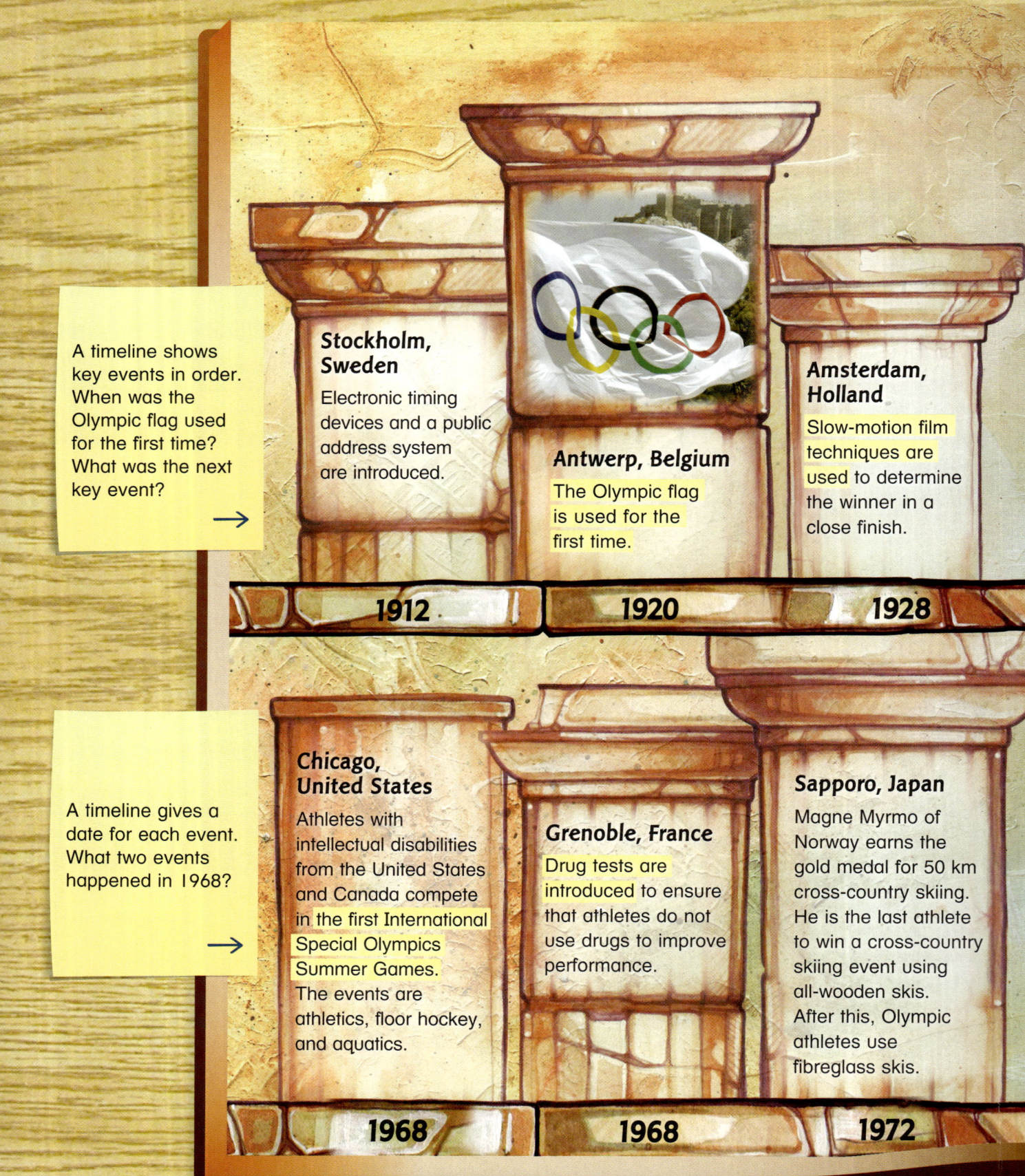

Berlin, Germany
These Olympics are the first sports competitions to be televised live. The Games are shown on large screens across Berlin.

London, England
For the first time, the Games can be seen on home TVs, but only within the British Isles. However, very few people own a TV set.

Rome, Italy
The first Paralympics are held, just after the 1960 Olympics. Four hundred wheelchair athletes from 23 nations compete in archery, basketball, fencing, field events, snooker, swimming, and table tennis.

1936   **1948**   **1960**

Lake Placid, United States
Artificial snow is used for the first time.

Lausanne, Switzerland
The International Olympic Committee votes to allow corporate sponsorship in the Games. Corporate sponsors (for example, food or car companies) give athletes money and other support. In exchange, the athletes wear logos representing these companies.

Athens, Greece
The Olympics return to the country of the ancient Games. The Olympic flame travels to six of the seven continents.

1980   **1983**   **2004**

> A timeline shows the earliest event at the beginning and the most recent event at the end. What is the most recent event shown on this timeline? ←

When We Built the Trojan Horse

Written by Althea Papayanakis
Illustrated by Russ Daff

Applying Strategies

Text Features: Timelines

A timeline can give you a summary of key events. As you read the story of the Trojan Horse, use the timeline to help you understand the story. Remember that a timeline

- gives a date for each event
- shows key events in order
- shows the earliest event at the beginning and the most recent event at the end

GATHER AROUND, GRANDCHILDREN. I'LL TELL YOU ABOUT THE TIME WE BUILT THE TROJAN HORSE. IT WAS LONG, LONG AGO....

1 I SAILED TO TROY WITH MY FATHER—YOUR GREAT GRANDFATHER—AND HUNDREDS OF GREEK SOLDIERS. FATHER WAS A CARPENTER. HE HELPED BUILD THE SHIPS THAT SAILED TO TROY.

2 WHEN WE GOT TO TROY, FATHER AND I HELPED BUILD THE PALISADE THE GREEK ARMY HID BEHIND. I WAS HIS APPRENTICE AND SOMEDAY I WOULD BE A BUILDER, TOO.

TIMELINE OF EVENTS IN THE TROJAN WAR

Before the War (around 1200 BCE)				The War Begins
▸ Helen, the wife of King Menelaus (men-eh-LAY-us) of Sparta (Greece), is kidnapped by Paris, the son of King Priam of Troy.	▸ King Menelaus asks his brother Agamemnon (ah-gah-MEM-non) for help.	▸ Agamemnon recruits other Greek leaders to join in the attack against Troy.	▸ Odysseus (oh-DEECE-ee-us) and Achilles (ah-KILL-eez), two powerful Greek leaders, agree to join forces with Agamemnon.	▸ Large Greek fleet sails toward Troy.

88 Early Civilizations

3 WE FOUGHT THE TROJANS FOR 10 YEARS! FOR 10 LONG YEARS WE SAT OUTSIDE THE WALLS OF TROY, NOT ABLE TO GET INSIDE TO DEFEAT THE TROJANS. WE WERE TIRED. WE MISSED OUR FAMILIES. WHEN WOULD THE WAR END?

4 AFTER 10 YEARS, FOOD WAS RUNNING LOW. MANY OF THE SOLDIERS WERE DYING FROM ILLNESS. I CARRIED WATER AND FOOD TO THE SICK. I WATCHED THE GREAT ACHILLES DIE FROM AN ARROW WOUND TO HIS HEEL.

5 WE WERE DESPERATE. FINALLY, ODYSSEUS, THE GREAT GREEK HERO, THOUGHT OF A PLAN TO DEFEAT TROY. THE FIRST PART OF THE PLAN WAS TO BUILD A GIGANTIC WOODEN HORSE ON WHEELS.

6 MY FATHER AND THE OTHER CARPENTERS WERE CALLED TOGETHER. IT TOOK MANY WEEKS TO BUILD THE HORSE.

(around 1190 BCE)	Ending the War (around 1180 BCE)			After the War
▶ Greeks battle Trojans and neighbouring regions for 9 years, but cannot break through the walls of Troy.	▶ Achilles and Paris are killed in battle in the 10th year.	▶ Odysseus comes up with a plan to build the Trojan horse.	▶ Troy is defeated and destroyed.	▶ Helen is reunited with King Menelaus.

7 THE FINISHED HORSE WAS AS TALL AS THE WALLS OF TROY. A PERSON ON A REAL HORSE COULD RIDE BENEATH THE BELLY OF THIS WOODEN HORSE. INSIDE, THE WOODEN HORSE WAS HOLLOW. ODYSSEUS AND 50 SOLDIERS HID INSIDE THE HORSE.

8 THE NEXT PART OF ODYSSEUS'S PLAN WAS TO TRICK THE TROJANS INTO BELIEVING WE HAD GONE. THOSE OF US NOT HIDING IN THE HORSE SAILED AWAY FROM TROY, BUT NOT TOO FAR.

9 WE ALSO LEFT BEHIND ONE OTHER MAN, SINON. THE PLAN WAS FOR SINON TO PRETEND HE HAD BEEN ABANDONED IN THE CHAOS OF LEAVING. HE WAS TO TELL THE TROJANS THAT THE HORSE WAS THE GREEKS' GIFT TO THE GODDESS ATHENA. ODYSSEUS HOPED THE TROJANS WOULD PULL THE HORSE TO THEIR TEMPLE TO ATHENA.

10 THE TROJANS DID JUST AS ODYSSEUS SAID THEY WOULD! THEY ROLLED THE WOODEN HORSE INTO THE CITY. THE TROJANS EVEN HAD TO TEAR DOWN SOME OF THE WALL TO GET THE HORSE INSIDE.

Staying on Topic

When you think of a great topic to write about, you usually have a lot to say. Ideas seem to fly onto the page. Often, some of those ideas are not closely related to the topic you started to write about.

Writing that has many ideas and no clear topic is difficult to read. As you read the paragraph below, try to figure out the writer's topic.

MY TRIP TO POMPEII

by Allie

August 24, 79 CE, started out like any other summer day in Pompeii, Italy. Nobody knew Mount Vesuvius was about to erupt and bury the town and everyone in it. I got to see Pompeii last summer when I visited my Uncle Nello in Naples. We had pizza and gelato, and we took lots of pictures. Uncle Nello explained to me that Pompeii is a town frozen in time. Everything in that city in 79 CE was preserved under a thick layer of hardened volcanic ash until Pompeii was excavated in the 1700s. It was very hot and I was glad I brought my hat. Luckily, I left my backpack behind because it was a sweaty kind of day—over 30 degrees! We strolled through the town centre, called the forum, and through people's homes. We saw food that was nearly 2000 years old—eggs, bread, walnuts, dates, figs, and olives. I've had a chance to try some of these foods for the first time on my trip. Uncle Nello loves to cook. Pompeii showed me how ancient Romans lived, but it was a dog that made me feel like I knew them. Just past someone's front door was a mosaic of a tough-looking dog. The dog's paws were draped over these words in Latin: *cave canem*. Uncle Nello translated: "Beware the Dog." I could just about hear that dog bark!

Allie asked a peer editor to read her paragraph. Read Allie's revised paragraph, and then figure out what Allie's editor suggested.

Visiting Ancient Pompeii
by Allie

August 24, 79 CE, started out like any other summer day in Pompeii, Italy. Nobody knew Mt. Vesuvius was about to erupt and bury the town and everyone in it. I got to see Pompeii last summer when I visited my Uncle Nello in Naples. Uncle Nello explained to me that Pompeii is a town frozen in time. Everything in the city in 79 CE was preserved under a thick layer of hardened volcanic ash until Pompeii was excavated in the 1700s. We strolled through the town centre, called the forum, and through people's homes. We saw food that was nearly 2000 years old—eggs, bread, walnuts, dates, figs, and olives. Pompeii showed me how ancient Romans lived, but it was a dog that made me feel like I knew them. Just past someone's front door was a mosaic of a tough-looking dog. The dog's paws were draped over these words in Latin: *cave canem*. Uncle Nello translated: "Beware the Dog." I could just about hear that dog bark!

How to Stay on Topic:

☑ Write down your topic before you begin writing.

☑ Think about your readers. Ask yourself, "Will my readers be able to identify the topic?"

☑ Revise your draft. Cross out anything that is not related to your topic.

☑ Read your revised draft out loud. Ask yourself, "Am I sticking to my topic?"

Discovering the Truth about Troy

by Emily Little

Applying Strategies

Reading Like a Writer
As you read this article, figure out the writer's topic. When you finish reading, look back at each paragraph. Ask yourself, "Did the writer stay on topic?"

It is 800 BCE, several hundred years after the Trojan War. A Greek poet named Homer decides to retell the stories he has heard about the war. There are so many and everyone in Greece loves to hear them. Homer creates a long poem, called the *Iliad,* about the Trojan War. Homer tells about the heroes of the war—Odysseus, Agamemnon, Achilles, and many others. He describes the battles on the plain outside Troy. Homer tells how Helen and the goddess Athena were involved in the war.

Archaeologist Heinrich Schliemann called this collection of artifacts "Priam's Treasure" after the Trojan king in Homer's *Iliad*. Experts later proved that this treasure was hundreds of years older than the Trojan War.

94 Early Civilizations

Around 1870 CE, a German archaeologist named Heinrich Schliemann reads the *Iliad*. It is the oldest piece of Greek writing that still exists. By now, all traces of Troy have disappeared. Many people think that Homer made up the story. Heinrich believes that there really was a city called Troy, and he decides to find it.

Heinrich goes to Turkey. From clues in the *Iliad*, he locates the hill where Troy was probably built. To the west, the sea sparkles in the sunlight. To the east, the dusty plain stirs in the wind.

Heinrich begins digging. Many people laugh at him. Still, Heinrich believes he will find Troy … and in 1870 he does!

Archaeologists have uncovered at least nine layers of ruins at the Troy site, dating from about 3000 BCE to 400 CE.

He not only discovers the great stone wall that surrounded the city of Troy, he finds many other things too—treasures of silver and gold and bronze. He finds the bones of humans and horses. He finds a gold crown. Troy did exist! The war that Homer wrote about was real!

There are many things mentioned in the poem that Heinrich does not find—a statue of Athena, chariots, the wooden horse that the Greeks hid within. These things are gone forever. The story of the wooden horse—handed down for nearly 3000 years—remains.

Reflect on

Writer's Craft: What was the writer's topic? Find three sentences that help you understand the topic.

Connections: Think about very old stories you know. Which ones do you think might be true? What makes you think so?

HOW WE

Written by Chris Rice and Melanie Rice
Illustrated by June Lawrason

Putting It All Together

As you read this article, remember to use the strategies you've learned in this unit:
- Make predictions.
- Use the timeline to help you understand.
- Identify the writer's topic.

Clues from the past

How do we know about past civilizations? We use clues found in buildings, paintings, written documents, books, and all sorts of objects that people leave behind—from tools to toys. As buildings are built or destroyed, objects lost hundreds of years ago are buried deep underground. Archaeologists dig for these objects. Historians examine the clues left behind to learn what life might have been like long ago in different parts of the world. What they learn is passed along to us through books and museum exhibits.

The Aztecs were a people who existed in North America about 500 years ago. The girl you are going to read about is imaginary, but her story is based on facts pieced together from objects and other clues found in Mexico.

An archaeologist examines the site where one of 14 stone carvings was found in the archaeological area of the Templo Mayor in Mexico City's main square.

96 Early Civilizations

LIVED

Growing up in Aztec Mexico

It is the year 1500 in North America, but in the calendar Xochitl [shah-CHE-tl] uses it is 8 Flint. Xochitl lives in a village on the shore of a lake. Her family farm stands across the water on an artificial island built with fertile mud from the lake.

Hello. My name is Xochitl. I'm an Aztec girl from long ago. I'm just ten, but I work hard every day. I help my family by preparing food. That's not all....

Innovations through time

| Around 6000 BCE | • DUGOUT CANOE | 5000 BCE | • GRINDING STONE
• LOOM |

heavy stone roller to grind corn

dried corn kernels

Xochitl helps with the work around her family home. Her mother grinds corn into flour on a grinding stone, while Xochitl makes tortillas for the family dinner. The tortillas are filled with vegetables grown on the family farm.

Every morning I roll up our bed blankets and sweep the floor. I pick corn with other girls in the village and bring it home to grind into flour. I pat the dough into tortillas.

Innovations mentioned in this article appeared in many civilizations across the globe. In this timeline, the approximate first date the innovation appeared has been given.

3000 BCE
- ARTIFICIAL ISLANDS
- PAPER (PAPYRUS)

800 BCE
- FLUTE

Xochitl also makes clothes with her mother. They weave thread into cloth using a wooden back-strap loom. The thread they use is made from cactus fibre, spun on a spindle. Thorns from the *maguey* (a type of cactus) make perfect pins and needles for weaving and sewing. Xochitl's long blouse, skirt, and shoes are made of cactus fibre.

The loom bar is attached to a tree or post.

Long threads are called the warp.

A weaving sword is used to smooth down weft threads.

Weft threads run under and over the warp threads.

A strap fits around the weaver's waist.

spindle with thread spun around it

cactus needles

My sister and I spin cactus fibre on a spindle to make the thread. My mother then weaves the thread into cloth. We use the cactus thorns for pins and needles. We have to be very careful not to stab our fingers on the sharp thorns.

Xochitl's father collects maguey leaves to make paper and thread. The men in the family are responsible for working their farm on the artificial island. The crops they grow include corn, tomatoes, chili peppers, and avocados.

Xochitl's people believe that one day the sun will die and the crops will not grow, but today the sun is in the sky. Xochitl gives thanks.

Every day, my father and brothers travel across the lake by canoe to reach our farm on the island. One of my brothers plays his flute for the corn goddess, so that she will help the crops grow.

Clues for tomorrow

When you lose an object, throw it away, or pass it on to someone else, think about how long that object might survive. What clues will it give to people who might find it in the future? Think about what life today will look like in the history books and museums of tomorrow.

Reflect on

Strategies: Which strategy helped you the most to understand what you were reading?

Your Learning: The author created an imaginary character to help you understand Aztec culture. Do you like this approach to learning history, or would you prefer plain facts? Explain.

Health

Making Choices

In this unit, you will
- identify the main idea and supporting details while you read
- identify characteristics of cause-and-effect text pattern
- choose effective organizational patterns for writing
- identify the main idea and supporting details while you listen
- identify overt and implied messages in ads
- learn about healthy living

Spot six people making healthy choices in this food court.

Understanding reading strategies

Finding Important Ideas

Finding important ideas helps you remember what you read. When you know the important ideas, you can identify supporting details that increase your understanding.

Use the title and headings to identify a purpose for reading. What do you expect to learn by reading this article?

Figure out how the article is organized. Each section in this article has a topic heading, a myth, and a fact. What is the important idea in this section?

Food Smarts
Myths and Facts

from *PBS Kids*

When it comes to healthy eating, you probably hear a lot of opinions and facts from your friends, relatives, and teachers. See if you know the truth behind these common myths.

Skipping Meals

Myth: As long as I skip a meal, I can eat whatever I want at my next meal.

to eat three normal-sized and healthy meals a day, and even a few snacks in between, so your body has energy when it needs it.

104 Making Choices

All Natural Labels

Myth: As long as a food package says "all natural" on it, the food is healthy.

Fact: Even if something is labelled "all natural," it can still have lots of sugars, fats, or other things that can be bad for you. Some snacks labelled "all natural" can have just as much sugars or fats as a chocolate bar! It's important to read the package, where the Nutrition Facts label and ingredients list will spell it all out for you.

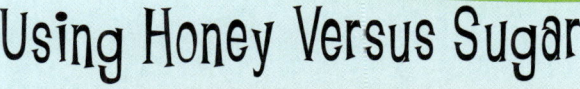

Using Honey Versus Sugar

Myth: I can sweeten my food as much as I want, as long as I use honey instead of sugar.

Fact: Chemically, honey is almost the same as sugar, and honey can even have more calories than sugar. Use honey just like you do sugar: only in small amounts.

> The important idea is often found in the first or last sentence in a section. What is the important idea in this section?

> Figure out how the article is organized. What important idea do you expect to read in this section? What do you learn?

Sugar Is a Good Source of Energy

Myth: Sugar gives you energy. If you need a boost mid-afternoon or before playing sports, eat a chocolate bar.

Fact: "Simple" sugars like those found in chocolate, cookies, candies, and cakes definitely cause spikes in your blood-sugar level, which may make you feel a quick shot of energy in your system. But after that first rush, blood sugar drops sharply, and you'll suddenly feel like you have less energy than before!

Fast Food

Myth: A fast-food cheeseburger is a balanced meal, because it has meat, cheese, bread, and vegetables.

Fact: Fast-food cheeseburgers, and many other foods served at fast-food restaurants, are very high in fats, calories, and sodium. It is okay to enjoy these foods once in a while, but if you're eating them a couple of times a week or more, this is too much, and you might want to try making healthier choices.

> Supporting details help you understand the important ideas. What supporting details explain why a cheeseburger isn't always the best choice for a meal?

FEED ME

from *yourSELF* Magazine

Applying Strategies

Finding Important Ideas

As you read this article, find important ideas to help you remember and understand what you are reading.

- Use the title and headings to identify a purpose for reading.
- Figure out how the article is organized.
- Check the first or last sentence in a section for the important idea.
- Identify supporting details.

Making Food Choices

To be your best, there are lots of things to think about. Two important things are *what* and *how much* you eat. All foods supply nutrients (substances your body needs to grow, have energy, and stay healthy), so *all foods* can be part of a healthful pattern of eating. There are no good or bad foods, but there are good or bad eating patterns. It's the total amount and the types of foods you eat over several days that make the difference. Choose a variety of foods for their different combinations of nutrients.

VARIETY	MODERATION	BALANCE
Try Different Foods for Their Great Tastes	**Eat All Kinds of Food, Just Go Easy on Amounts**	**Make Food Choices Count Over Several Days**
Eating a variety of foods boosts your chances of getting the many nutrients your body needs to grow strong and healthy.	You don't need to measure everything you eat. However, watching how much you eat helps you get enough variety and not overdo it on any one specific food or food group. As often as possible, choose foods that are low in sugars and fats.	Balancing food choices over several days helps you get enough of the nutrients you need. Eat enough servings from Canada's Food Guide each day.

Snack Attack

You're hungry. Again. Your stomach is grumbling. You reach for the only thing that will quiet the rumbling—a snack. But what's the deal? Why do you seem to be so hungry all the time? You're growing. Your body needs extra energy and nutrients from food. So quiet the grumble and rumble: eat a snack. Now, read on for some tips to help your snack be tops.

SNACK FACT 1

Pick snacks to fill your Food Guide gaps:
- Hit your day's Grain Group target by snacking on a bagel, pretzels, popcorn, muffin, breakfast cereal, or oatmeal cookies.

- If your day's meals come up short on the Vegetable and Fruit Groups, reach for crunchy raw vegetables, frozen fruit-juice bars, dried fruit, or a piece of whole fruit.

- Short on the Milk Group? Guzzle a glass of milk or grab string cheese, a carton of reduced-fat yogurt, or a scoop of frozen yogurt.

- If you have a gap in the Meat and Alternatives Group, try a hard-boiled egg, a slice of lean meat, or a handful of peanuts.

EAT LESS
fats and sweets, which just add extra calories and provide little or no nutrition.

- frozen treats • candy • soft drinks • cake • cream cheese

EAT ENOUGH
low-fat dairy foods for calcium and enough lean meats or beans for iron.

- milk • beans • yogurt • cottage cheese • beef • peanut butter • nuts

EAT MORE
fruits and vegetables than you're used to eating.

- juice • raisins • melons • berries • grapes • mangoes • peaches • bok choy
- bean sprouts

EAT PLENTY
of breads, cereals, rice, and pasta as your best foods for energy.

- whole-grain cereals • tortillas • pasta • brown or wild rice

SNACK FACT 2

Take time to enjoy your snacks, as well as your meals. It takes a while for your brain to know your stomach is full. Slow down, eat, and enjoy.

SNACK FACT 3

Make snack drinks count toward food-group servings. Drink milk, fruit juice, or a shake made with fruit, ice cubes, and milk (not ice cream).

SNACK FACT 4

Use food labels to make smart snack choices. The nutrition facts tell you the calories, fats, sugars, and other nutrients in one serving.

- bacon • chocolate • butter • salad dressing
- eggs • baked fish • skinless chicken • ham
- broccoli • baked potatoes • tomatoes • okra
- pitas • low-fat muffins • oatmeal

Try This!

Check Nutrition Facts

Thirsty? Which of these drinks would you choose: pop or juice? As you think about your choice, look at the nutrition facts on the food labels. Which drink do you choose for Vitamin C?

Pop

Nutrition Facts	
Serving Size 354 mL	
Amount Per Serving	
Calories 140	
	% of Daily Value*
Total Fat 0 g	0%
Sodium 50 mg	2%
Total Carbohydrates 39 g	13%
Sugars 39 g	
Protein 0 g	

* Percent of Daily Values are based on a 2000 calorie diet.

Orange Juice

Nutrition Facts	
Serving Size 240 mL	
Amount Per Serving	
Calories 130	
	% of Daily Value*
Total Fat 0 g	0%
Saturated Fat 0 g	0%
Cholesterol 0 mg	0%
Sodium 0 mg	0%
Potassium 450 mg	13%
Total Carbohydrates 26 g	9%
Dietary Fibre 0 g	0%
Sugars 22 g	
Protein 2 g	
Vitamin A 0% • Vitamin C	120%
Calcium 2% • Iron	0%
Thiamin 10% • Niacin	4%
Vitamin B 6% • Folate	15%

* Percent of Daily Values are based on a 2000 calorie diet. Your daily values may be higher or lower depending on your calorie needs.

Reflect on

Strategies: How did the organization of this article help you to find important ideas?

Connections: What did you learn about your own food choices? What will change and what will stay the same about your eating habits?

Identifying Characteristics of Cause-and-Effect Text Pattern

Writers use cause-and-effect text pattern to answer the question "why?" Cause-and-effect text pattern has certain characteristics:

- Ideas are linked to show that one thing (the cause) makes something else (the effect) happen.
- One cause can have several effects.
- One effect can have several causes.

Ideas are linked to show that one thing (the cause) makes something else (the effect) happen. What happens if you drink water?

WILD ABOUT WATER

by Rohan Siharath

You've just drunk a glass of water. That's good because water is the most important nutrient for your body. In fact, drinking water keeps you alive.

What does water do for your body? Water is the main ingredient in the fluids running through your body. Fluids carry nutrients to, and waste from, all of your organs and cells. For you to live, your heart, brain, lungs, intestines, and all other parts of your body need these fluids.

Making Choices

WATER IN YOUR BLOOD ... AND OTHER FLUIDS

Water is the main ingredient in your blood and the juices in your digestive system. Because your body has water in it, you are able to

- digest that burger and fries you ate for lunch
- get rid of stuff your body doesn't need through liquid waste (urine)
- control your body temperature by sweating (perspiring)

WATER MOVES YOUR JOINTS

If an object like a door squeaks, some oil rubbed on the hinges will help the hinges move easily. Water works this way, too. Water is the main ingredient in the fluid that lubricates the joints in your body. Joints are the parts of the body where your bones connect, like your elbows.

WATER MAKES WASTE MOVE

The food you eat has to move through your body. Having water in your body helps you move the digested food through your intestines and get rid of the waste products of digestion (the stuff your body doesn't need).

One cause can have several effects. What are three important effects of drinking water?

←

←

Ideas are linked to show that one thing (the cause) makes something else (the effect) happen. What effect does water have on your joints and digestive system?

←

WATER KEEPS YOU COOL

Your normal body temperature should be about 37 °C. Without water, when you exercise or play, or even just sit around in hot weather, your body would become too hot. With the help of water, if your body becomes too hot, it can cool down. Your body cools down by producing perspiration. The perspiration leaves your skin through tiny holes called *pores*. When the sweat hits the air, it evaporates and you cool down.

DRINK LOTS OF WATER!

You can see that your body uses lots of water. But it's important to note that on a normal day your body loses enough water to fill a 2-L bottle. By drinking water, and some other liquids, you can replace the water your body loses. Eating is another way to replace water. Most foods, especially fruits and vegetables, have some water in them.

Water is wonderful! Let it work for you to help you digest food, move around easily, get rid of waste, and cool down.

→ One effect can have several causes. What helps your body cool down?

→ Ideas are linked to show that one thing (the cause) makes something else (the effect) happen. What is the effect of drinking water?

DRINK UP

by Patrick Peters

We all know that drinking water is good for us. What about other liquids, such as milk, juice, pop, or coffee and tea? Can these liquids help you get back the water that you lose every day?

Applying Strategies

Identifying Characteristics of Cause-and-Effect Text Pattern

As you read, look for these characteristics of cause-and-effect text pattern:

- Ideas are linked to show that one thing (the cause) makes something else (the effect) happen.
- One cause can have several effects.
- One effect can have several causes.

Milk

When you're really thirsty, a glass of cold milk goes down just as smoothly as a glass of cold water. Milk is a great thirst-quencher. It has other benefits, too. In order to grow strong bones and teeth, kids need calcium. Milk is a good source of this mineral. Milk is also a source of protein, which is important in developing the brain and helps in the growth of body tissues.

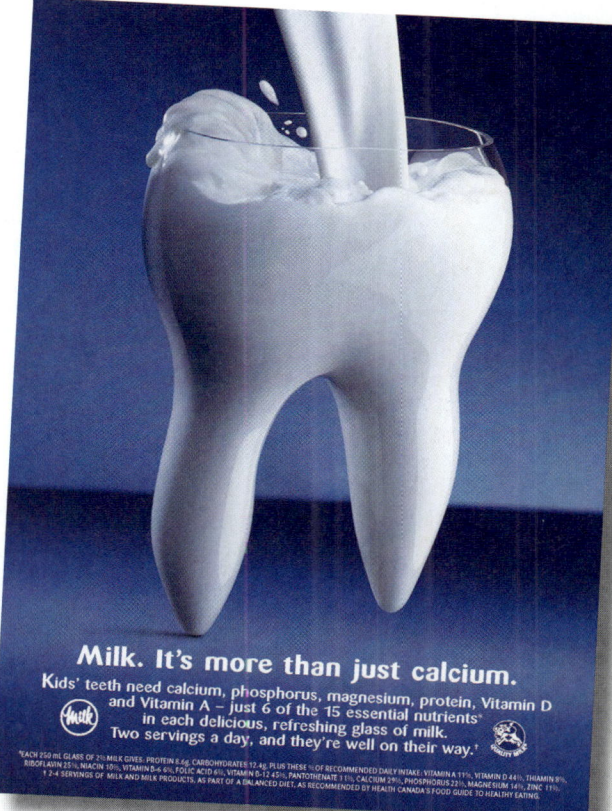

Juice

Juice is a good replacement for water, too. Choose 100% fruit juice because it's a natural source of nutrients and vitamins. Watch out for the natural sugar in juice, though. If you have juice often, cut down on the sugar by mixing half water and half juice.

Pop

Pop is not a good replacement for water because it usually contains stuff your body doesn't need, such as sugar (or artificial sweeteners), caffeine, or other chemicals (such as artificial flavours). Caffeine is a natural chemical found in tea leaves, coffee beans, cacao beans (the stuff used to make chocolate), and kola nuts (the plant that gives cola its flavour). For more on why caffeine should be avoided, see the next section.

Coffee and Tea

You might think that tea and coffee are good drink choices because they contain water. The concern with coffee and tea is the caffeine in them. Drinks with caffeine cause you to urinate more often than usual. That's not good because you need to replace water, not lose it!

Another effect of caffeine is that it can boost your energy for a short time. While caffeine can make you feel more awake, you should avoid drinks with caffeine because the caffeine can make you feel nervous and jumpy. Too much caffeine may also cause headaches, stomachaches, and a racing heartbeat.

Reflect on

Strategies: How did identifying the characteristics of cause-and-effect text pattern help you find the important ideas in this article?

Critical Literacy: Why would companies selling milk, juice, pop, coffee, or tea want their customers to read this article? Why might they hope customers don't read it?

Understanding media

Making Inferences Using Overt and Implied Messages

Fun Food Ads

Successful ads are a creative mix of overt and implied messages. Whether you want yummy treats or cooler clothes, advertisers have a message for you.

You can have fun reading ads and trying to figure out how the ads are "working." Ask yourself, "What are the messages? What can I infer from these messages? Is this a successful ad?"

An implied message gives you a feeling. For example, some advertisers imply that you'll look cool if you use their products. What feelings do the cartoons and words in this ad give you?

Milk mustaches don't last long when you're a sponge.

Which means I may have to drink another glass of yummy chocolate milk.

Or two.

Or three.

Or four.

CHOCOLATE got milk?

An overt message tells you something directly. What words tell you about the product this advertiser is selling?

Combine overt and implied messages and your own ideas to make inferences. What does this ad want you to infer about chocolate milk? Is it successful?

Can you figure out how this ad is working? Identify the overt and implied messages, and then make inferences about what the advertiser wants you to think or do.

Understanding Writing Strategies

Choosing an Organizational Pattern

Writers can choose different ways to organize their writing. Choosing an organizational text pattern that matches your purpose helps readers understand your message.

These writers are working together on a newsletter about exercise. Each writer has decided on a purpose for writing. Notice how the writers have chosen different organizational text patterns.

How to choose an organizational pattern:

- ✓ Decide on your purpose for writing.
- ✓ Consider several different organizational text patterns.
- ✓ Choose the organizational text pattern that will help your readers understand your message.

FOOD-AD TRICKS

from *Zillions® Magazine, Consumer Reports® for Kids*

Applying Strategies
Reading Like a Writer
As you read this article, identify the organizational pattern the writer chose and think about how this pattern helps the writer communicate a message.

What does a dash of Vaseline have to do with a burger commercial? It's part of the burger's makeup! Just like any TV celebrity, this plump and pampered star spent hours in makeup and wardrobe so it would look its mouth-watering best under the camera's hot lights! It may look very different in real life. In fact, many delicious foods you see on TV may not be so appetizing once you find out what's really happening behind the scenes.

BUILD A YUMMY TV BURGER

It takes hours of hard work, and plenty of clever tricks, to make a fast-food burger look good enough to eat. We went on the set of a burger commercial to capture the step-by-step action. (Warning: the truth may spoil your appetite!)

STEP 1

Fry for 20 s on each side. The burger is still raw inside, and it's not safe to eat, but it looks cooked on camera. That's what counts, say food stylists (makeup artists who are experts with food). A fully cooked burger would shrink and look too dark.

STEP 2

Strike with a hot skewer to give the burger "grill" lines for that fresh-from-the-barbecue look.

STEP 3

Brush with brown food dye, vegetable oil, or Vaseline. The burger will have a juicy shine.

STEP 4

Cut a slit in the back of the burger.

STEP 5

Spread out the burger so it doesn't look so scrawny. Remember, the camera shoots only the burger's "best side" (the front). You'd never know the burger is not really as big as it seems on TV, until now!

STEP 6

Sort through thousands of buns to find one that's big and fluffy. "Not too dark, too light, too squished, or too wrinkled," say food stylists. "It may take all day."

STEP 7

Glue on extra sesame seeds for a full, finished look.

STEP 8
Place a cardboard liner between the burger and the bottom bun. That keeps the greasy patty from sinking into the bun.

STEP 9
Sort through dozens of heads of lettuce for a piece that looks cool and refreshing. (The lettuce is kept in ice water on the set so it stays extra crispy.) Pin the lettuce into place on the burger.

STEP 10
Pin on a tomato slice. Place a plastic liner beneath the tomato so the juice doesn't run and get the bun soggy.

Reflect on

Strategies: Why do you think the writer chose this organizational pattern? What other organizational pattern might work well to communicate this message?

Critical Literacy: Do you think companies that use "food-ad tricks" are lying to consumers, or are they just doing what is necessary to produce an appealing ad?

Understanding listening strategies

Identifying Main Ideas While Listening

Most of the time when you listen, you don't have a pencil and paper handy, and you won't have a chance to hear the message again. You can remember what's important if you distinguish between main ideas and supporting details. Listen for the main ideas and don't worry about the details.

These students are enjoying a fitness assembly. The speakers are top athletes. Notice how listening for main ideas helps some listeners understand what they are hearing.

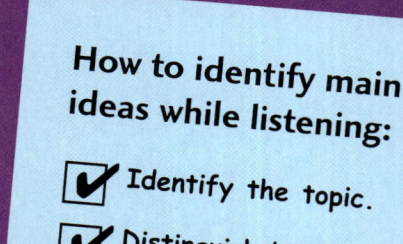

How to identify main ideas while listening:

☑ Identify the topic.

☑ Distinguish between main ideas and supporting details.

☑ Repeat the main ideas in your head so you remember them.

122 Making Choices

Putting It All Together

As you read, remember to use the strategies you learned in this unit:
- Find important ideas.
- Identify characteristics of cause-and-effect text pattern.

THE RIGHT TO RESIST

Pressure is the feeling that you are being pushed toward a certain choice—good or bad. If someone is pressuring you to do anything that's not right or good for you, then you have the right to resist. You have the right to say "no," the right not to give a reason why, and the right to just walk away from a situation.

Resisting pressure can be hard for some people. Why? They …

- are afraid of being rejected by others
- want to be liked and don't want to lose a friend
- don't want to be made fun of
- don't want to hurt someone's feelings
- aren't sure of what they really want
- don't know how to get out of the situation

Sometimes resisting others isn't easy, but you can resist anything you may feel pressured into with practice and a little know-how.

Quick Tips on Resisting Pressure

If you try these tips, you will find it easier to resist pressure. Copy them and stash them somewhere safe where you can peek at them when you need a reminder.

Quick Tips
- Say "no" and make it clear that you mean it.
- Stand up straight.
- Make eye contact.
- Say how you feel.
- Don't make excuses.
- Stick up for yourself.

Resisting Spoken Pressure

Spoken pressure (when someone pressures you with words) can be difficult to resist. Most people don't want to risk making others feel bad, but it's important to stand up for yourself. Check out these strategies for dealing with spoken pressure.

Do …	Don't …
• say "no" assertively	• be afraid to say "no"
• suggest something else to do	• mumble
• stand up for others	• say "no" too aggressively
• walk away from the situation	• act like a know-it-all when saying "no"
• find something else to do	

RETURN THE CHALLENGE. MAYBE SAY, "I THOUGHT YOU WERE MY FRIEND."

… OR, "I DON'T WANT TO SMOKE AND IF YOU'RE MY FRIEND YOU WON'T ASK ME TO."

Being assertive means
- standing up straight
- looking directly at the person
- speaking in a firm voice
- choosing words well (instead of a wimpy "I can't," say, "I don't want to")

Know How to Say "NO!"

If you want to resist, then you'll need to stay in control of the situation, and of course, stay free of whatever the pressure may be. You can say "no" many different ways, but one way is more effective than the rest.

This is an aggressive answer. It is not the most effective way to say "no."

This is a passive answer. It is not the most effective way to say "no."

This is an avoiding answer. It is not the most effective.

This is a know-it-all answer. It is not the most effective.

This is an assertive answer. It is the most effective.

Resisting Unspoken Pressure

Sometimes you can feel pressure just from watching how others act or dress, without them saying a word to you. This "unspoken pressure" may come from role models such as your parents, your older siblings, teachers, coaches, or celebrities you see in movies and on TV. Unspoken pressure may also come from your friends or other people your age.

Here are some tips for resisting unspoken pressure when others are pressuring you to do something you know is wrong:

- Take a reality check—not everyone is behaving this way.
- Walk away from the situation.
- Find something else to do with other friends.

Resisting pressure isn't easy, but now you have some ideas about how to resist and make choices that are right for you.

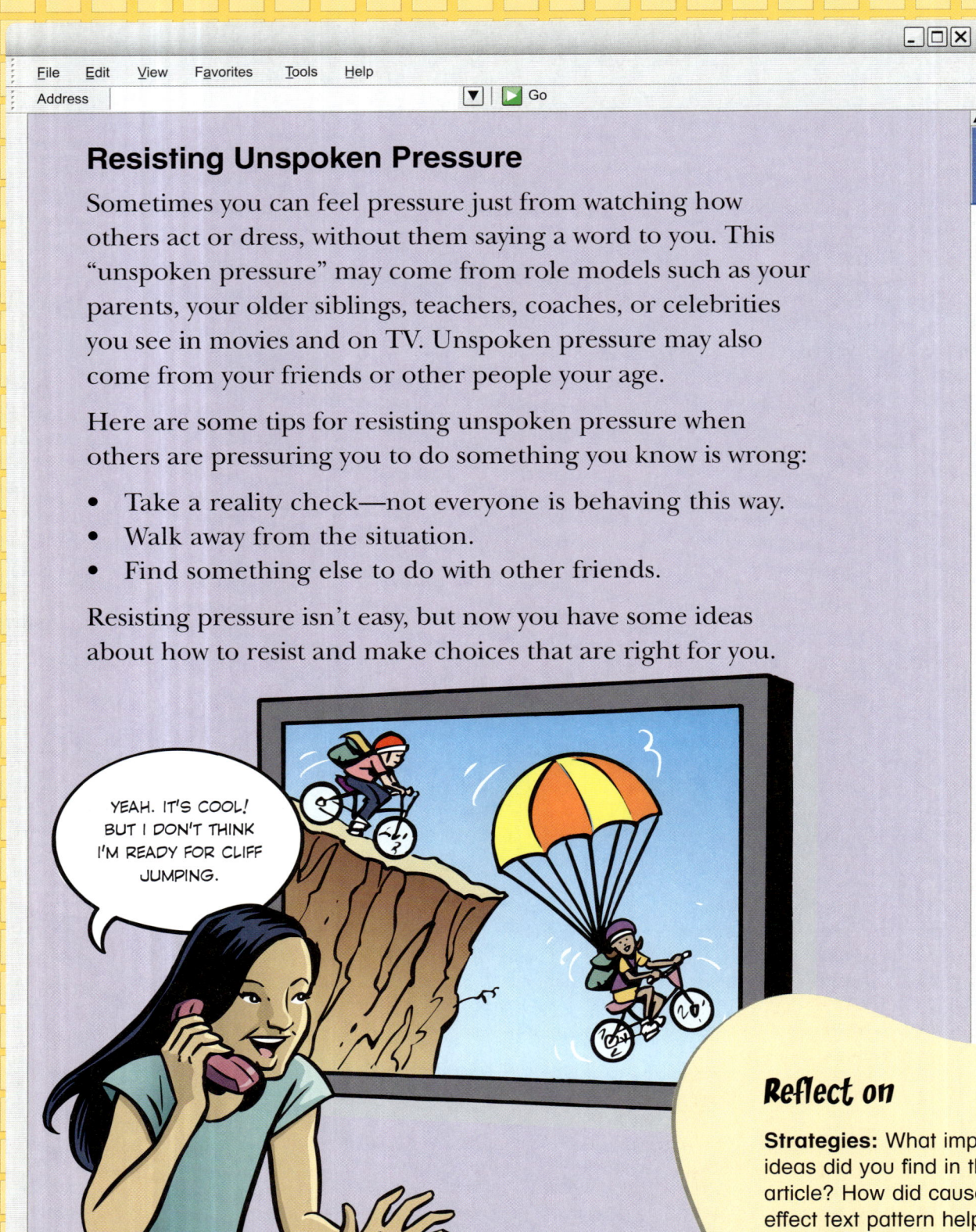

Reflect on

Strategies: What important ideas did you find in the article? How did cause-and-effect text pattern help you understand these ideas?

Your Learning: Find three ideas in this article that really made sense to you and that you'd like to remember.

Credits

Text

pp. 10–11: The Case of the Sneak Thief's Sneakers by Hy Conrad originally appeared on MysteryNet.com: "The Online Mystery Network." Copyright 1996, 2006 MysteryNet.com.; pp. 17–20: The Dirty Dog from *Super Sleuth: Twelve Solve-It-Yourself Mysteries* by Jackie Vivelo (New York: G.P. Putnam's Sons) 1985, 11–17; pp. 44–47: From *SPEEDY FACTS: YOU'RE TALL IN THE MORNING BUT SHORTER AT NIGHT* by Melvin and Gilda Berger. Copyright © 2003 by Melvin and Gilda Berger. Reprinted by permission of Scholastic Inc.; pp. 48–49: *Gross Universe: Your Guide to All Disgusting Things Under the Sun* by Jeff Szpirglas. Maple Tree Press Inc., 2004, pp. 8–11. With permission of the publisher, Maple Tree Press Inc., Toronto, Canada.; pp. 50–53: *It's All in Your Head* by Sylvia Funston and Jay Ingram. Maple Tree Press Inc., 2005, pp. 4–6. With permission of the publisher, Maple Tree Press Inc., Toronto, Canada.; pp. 54–55: *Bubble Facts... Human Body*. Miles Kelly Publishing Ltd., 2004. With kind permission from Miles Kelly Publishing Ltd.; pp. 60–63: By Rudy Garcia-Tolson as told to Elizabeth Deffner photographs by Joel Ball, from *National Geographic Kids*, December 2005/January 2006, pp. 34–36. Reprinted by permission.; pp. 65–68: From *What If: The Human Body* by Steve Parker, illustrated by Tony Kenyon. Aladdin Books Ltd., 1995. Reprinted by permission.; pp. 70–71: Reproduced from The Usborne Time Traveller Rome & the Romans by permission of Usborne Publishing, 83–85 Saffron Hill, London EC1N 8RT, UK. Distributed in the USA by EDC Publishing. Copyright © 2003, 1997, 1993, 1990, 1977 Usborne Publishing Ltd.; pp. 72–75: From *Ancient Egyptians* by Fiona MacDonald. Reprinted by permission of HarperCollins Publishers Ltd. © Fiona MacDonald, 2003.; pp. 76–79: Material from *Adventures In Ancient China* written by Linda Bailey and illustrated by Bill Slavin is used by permission of Kids Can Press Ltd., Toronto. Text © 2003 Linda Bailey Illustrations © 2003 Bill Slavin.; pp. 94–95: From THE TROJAN HORSE by Emily Little, illustrated by Michael Eagle, copyright © 1988 by Random House, Inc. Illustrations copyright © 1988 by Michael Eaglr. Used by permission of Random House Children's Books, a division of Random House, Inc.; pp. 96–100: Adapted from *How Children Lived* by Chris and Melanie Rice, Dirling Kindersley, 1995. Reproduced by permission of Penguin Books Ltd.; pp. 104–106: "It's My Life," PBS Kids © 2005 CastleWorks, Inc.; pp. 107–109: Adapted from *yourSELF* Magazine, Food and Nuitrition Service, U.S. Department of Agriculture.; pp. 118–121: "Food-Ad Tricks" Copyright 2000 by Consumers Union of U.S., Inc. Yonkers, NY 10703-1057, a nonprofit organization. Reprinted with permission from Zillions®: Consumer Reports 4 Kids for educational purposes only. No commercial use or reproduction permitted. <http://www.consumerreports.org/> www.ConsumerReports.org® and <http://www.consumerreports.org/classroom> www.consumerreports.org/classroom.; pp. 123–126: Reprinted with permission from the National Institute on Alcohol Abuse and Alcoholism, www.thecoolspot.gov.

Photos

Cover: Richard Nowitz/Getty Images, Philip Date/Shutterstock, Brand X Pictures/Jupiter Images.; p. 4: Robert Holmgren/Getty Images; p. 5: Emilia Stasiak/Shutterstock; p. 7: Image Source/Getty Images; pp. 10–11: Mark Yuill/Shutterstock; p. 34: (l) Book cover in the NANCY DREW SERIES ®, THE MOONSTONE CASTLE MYSTERY. NANCY DREW and all related characters and images are © and registered trademarks of Simon & Schuster, Inc. All rights reserved. The classic hardcover editions of these Nancy Drew titles are available from Grosset & Dunlap, an imprint of Penguin Books for Young Readers. Used by permission of Simon & Schuster Publishing. Copyright © 1963.; (r) Book cover in the HARDY BOYS SERIES ®, THE SECRET OF THE OLD MILL. HARDY BOYS and all related characters and images are © and registered trademarks of Simon & Schuster, Inc. All rights reserved. The classic hardcover editions of these Hardy Boys titles are available from Grosset & Dunlap, an imprint of Penguin Books for Young Readers. Used by permission of Simon & Schuster Adult Publishing Group. Copyright © 1927, 1962.; p. 35: (l) Nancy Drew: Pit of Vipers © 2006 Aladdin Paperbacks, an imprint of Simon & Schuster. Nancy Drew ® is a registered trademark of Simon & Schuster, Inc. All rights reserved. Used by permission of Simon and Schuster Publishing.; (r) Hardy Boys: Warehouse Rumble © 2004 Aladdin Paperbacks, an imprint of Simon & Schuster. Hardy Boys ® is a registered trademark of Simon & Schuster, Inc. All rights reserved. Used by permission of Simon and Schuster Publishing; p. 41: © Leo Mason/Corbis; p. 42: (bl) Chris Salvo/Getty Images, (tr) Melissa Dockstader/Shutterstock, (cr) PhotoLink/Photodisc/Getty Images, (br) michael ledray/Shutterstock, (c) © 2007 JupiterImages and its Licensors. All Rights Reserved; p. 43: (bl) Bobby Deal/RealDealPhoto/Shutterstock, (tr) Cristi Matei/Shutterstock, (cl) Don Farrall/Getty Images, (tl) Robert Holmgren/Getty Images, (c) Ryan McVay/Photodisc/Getty Images, (br) © 2007 JupiterImages and its Licensors. All Rights Reserved; p. 44: (c) Cristi Matei/Shutterstock, (b) © Dr. Dennis Kunkel/Visuals Unlimited, (t) © Dr. Kessel & Dr. Kardon/Tissues & Organs/ Visuals Unlimited; p. 45: (cr) Dr. Jeremy Burgess/Photo Researchers, Inc., (l) © Dr. Dennis Kunkel / Visuals Unlimited, (br) Dr. Jeremy Burgess/Photo Researchers, Inc., (t) © Dr. David M. Phillips/Visuals Unlimited; p. 46: (b) Ryan McVay/Photodisc/Getty Images, (t) Sebastian Kaulitzki/Shutterstock; p. 47: GEOFF TOMPKINSON/SCIENCE PHOTO LIBRARY; p. 60: Joel Ball; p. 61: (l) Joel Ball, (r) Joel Ball; pp. 62–63: Joel Ball; p. 63: Joel Ball; p. 69: Harald Sund/Getty Images; pp. 72–75: Albo/Shutterstock; p. 72: (cl) Bill McKelvie/Shutterstock, (r) Fragment of the Ebers Papyrus, New Kingdom, c.1550 BC (papyrus), Egyptian, 18th Dynasty (c.1567–1320 BC) / University Library, Leipzig, Germany, Archives Charmet / The Bridgeman Art Library, (bl) Rosetta Stone, c.196 BC (stone) (detail), Egyptian, Ptolemaic Period (332–30 BC) / British Museum, London, UK, © Boltin Picture Library / The Bridgeman Art Library; p. 73: Wall to Wall Television; p. 74: PHILIPPE PLAILLY / EURELIOS / SCIENCE PHOTO LIBRARY; p. 75: (t) ALEXANDER TSIARAS/SCIENCE PHOTO LIBRARY, (b) Wall to Wall Television; pp. 80–83: With permission of the Royal Ontario Museum © ROM; p. 81: (br) Miller Hare © ROM 2005. All rights reserved.; p. 84: (c) Erich Lessing/Art Resource, NY, (r) © Araldo de Luca/CORBIS; p. 85: Roger Viollet/Getty Images; p. 86: © Reuters/CORBIS; p. 87: (tr) AFP/Getty Images, (b) Ezra Shaw/Getty Images; (tl) Photo by Hulton Archive/Getty Images; p. 93: The Art Archive/Dagli Orti; p. 94: Photo by Rischgitz/Getty Images; p. 95: © Wolfgang Kaehler/CORBIS; p. 96: DANIEL AGUILAR/Reuters/Landov; p. 101: Toronto Star/First Light; p. 107: Emilia Stasiak/Shutterstock; pp. 110–112: Shutterstock; p. 113: Courtesy of Dairy Farmers of Canada. Photography: Philip Rostron - Instil Productions Inc.; p. 115: PRNewsFoto/National Dairy Council; p. 116: Courtesy of Nestle USA; p. 118: Maxim Kalmykov/Shutterstock; pp. 118–121: GJS/Shutterstock.

Art

pp 8–9: Brian McLachlan; pp. 12–16: Greg Ruhl; pp. 17–20: Kelly Kennedy; pp. 21–26: Greg Ruhl; p. 27: Brian McLachlan; pp. 28–33: Greg Ruhl; p. 36: Brian McLachlan; pp. 37–40: Greg Ruhl; pp. 48–49: Michael Cho; pp. 50–53: Bart Vallecoccia (brain art and background), Jason Bone (character); pp. 57–59: Greg Ruhl; p. 64: Steve Manale; p. 65: Vesna Krstanovic (girl at bottom); pp. 72–75: Allan Moon; pp. 76–79: Bill Slavin; pp. 84–87: Dave Kang; pp. 88–91: Russ Daff; pp. 96–100: June Lawrason; pp. 102–103: Piers Baker; pp. 104–106: Pat N. Lewis; pp. 108–109: Gwyneth Fatemi; p. 112: Dominic Bugatto; p. 114: Stacy Heller Budnick; p. 117: Jason Bone; p. 122: James Yamasaki; pp. 123–126: Paul Fricke/Blue Moon Studios.